Delight Ministries Delight Ministries Delight Ministries Delight Ministries Delight Ministries Delight Ministries Delight Ministries Delight Ministries Delight Ministries Delight Ministries Delight Ministries Delight Ministries

KNOWN

KNOW JESUS

KNOW WHO YOU ARE IN JESUS

MAKE JESUS KNOWN

Delight Ministries

A DELIGHT MINISTRIES STUDY

Delight Ministries
www.delightministries.com

Printed in the United States of America
First Printing: August 2021
Believers Press
ISBN: 978-1-7343272-2-9

Welcome!

Here we are! It's a new semester of Delight and we are soooo excited for what God has planned for the months to come. You might notice that this study is a little different from past *Delight Stories and Scripture* books. We are so passionate about the topic of Known that we are spending alllll semester diving into it. Throughout the course of this book, you will learn how to know Jesus, how to know who you are in Jesus, and how to make Jesus known. Each category has its own section containing Scripture teaching and a story from a Delight girl like you. Our prayer for this study is that you will have new wisdom and understanding about who God is and what that means for you.

Are you ready?!

Our Mission

Our mission is to invite college women into **Christ-centered community** that **fosters vulnerability** and **transforms stories.**

Christ-Centered Community

We launch, grow, and sustain thriving Christ-centered communities on college campuses. We've seen time and time again that community is often the catalyst for true Kingdom impact.

Foster Vulnerability

We aim to provide a space on college campuses for women to vulnerably share how Christ has been at work in their lives. We believe that vulnerability leads to breakthrough, and breakthrough leads to transformation!

Transform Stories

We believe that one moment with Jesus can truly change everything. Our mission is to give college women numerous opportunities to meet with Jesus and have their lives transformed!

Delight DNA

You are officially family if you are holding this book in your hands! We want you to know who we are at Delight so you can truly feel like a part of the fam! You can scan this code above to explore our brand new **Delight DNA site,** which was created for women just like you to understand more of our *heartbeat* as a ministry.

Within **Delight DNA**, Mac and Kenz share the story behind Delight and their vision for it today. We dive deeper into our Core Values and even share a five-day devo to help you incorporate them into your everyday life! Plus, we share more of our vision for this book you are holding and how to get the most out of it. We can't wait for you to check out this amazing resource and pray that it makes you feel connected to all of us here at Delight!

Table
of
Contents

01 *Week One:*
THE FATHER'S
HOUSE / Page 19

02 *Week Two:*
THE SHEPHERD'S
VOICE / Page 37

03 *Week Three:*
THE POSTURE OF
UNITY / Page 55

04 *Week Four:*
KEEP ASKING
/ Page 77

05 *Week Five:*
HIS TEMPTATION
STRATEGY
/ Page 95

06 *Week Six:*
SHARE YOUR
STORY / Page 113

07 *Week Seven:*
THE CROWDED
HEART / Page 119

08 *Week Eight:*
BE AN
INFLUENCER/
Page 139

09 *Week Nine:*
DON'T MISS
YOUR MOMENT
/ Page 157

10 *Week Ten:*
GO AND TELL
/ Page 175

How to Read this Book:

SCRIPTURE: Each week you'll start off with reading a passage of Scripture, anywhere from a few verses to a couple chapters. The chapters in this book will walk you through the reading process. As you read, you'll answer questions, fill in blanks, and hopefully get a deeper understanding of the context behind what you're reading. You'll want to pull out your Bible and start reading anytime you see something like this....

Go and read Matthew 6:22-23.

Just remember that gray highlights are your cue to pause and open the Word. Each week, we will zero in on one topic that the Scripture text introduces. Our prayer is that this book brings new light to Bible stories and verses that you've perhaps read a million times.

STORY: Each week you'll read the story of a REAL college girl or recent graduate. She will share how she has seen that week's Scripture text at work in her life. Our prayer is that you see yourself in the midst of each and every one of the stories and that you're able to begin to identify how God might be present in your story too.

CONVERSATION STARTERS: Our goal is to get the conversation rolling between you and the Lord, as well as within your Delight community. These 4 questions will help you do just that for every week! We suggest setting some time aside each week to answer these questions in a prayerful way with the Lord. Then, come ready to discuss them with your Delight community. The more time you take to prepare on the front end—the better your conversations will be!

Before we Begin:

One of my favorite moments from the life of Jesus comes from the Gospel of Matthew, chapter 16. Jesus took the disciples on a journey north to a place called Caesarea Philippi.

Caesarea Philippi was an ancient city about 20 miles from the region of Galilee, which was the home base of Jesus's ministry. Although it wasn't geographically that far from the Sea of Galilee, culturally it was miles apart! It was an ancient Roman city located at the base of Mount Hermon. Carved into the rock faces there were many depictions of idols and gods, the primary one being Pan, the God of sexuality.

At the base of this mountain was a huge cave that was referred to as the Gates of Hades because in the springtime, the increased rainfall would make the waters flow out of the cave. Many people believed that it was the demons and gods from the underworld making their entrance into the world. Crowds from all over the country would gather at this place engaging in all sorts of public sexual acts and immoralities as an homage to the god Pan.

Caesarea Philippi was anything but PG! You see, religious people *wouldn't be caught dead* there—but it was the very place where Jesus decided to take His disciples on a special field trip to ask them a few questions. Let's look at this moment together!

When Jesus came to the region of Caesarea Philippi, he asked his disciples, "Who do people say the Son of Man is?"

They replied, "Some say John the Baptist; others say Elijah; and still others, Jeremiah or one of the prophets."

"But what about you?" he asked. "Who do you say I am?"

Simon Peter answered, "You are the Messiah, the Son of the living God."

Jesus replied, "Blessed are you, Simon son of Jonah, for this was not revealed to you by flesh and blood, but by my Father in heaven. And I tell you that you are Peter, and on this rock I will build my church, and the gates of Hades will not overcome it. I will give you the keys of the kingdom of heaven; whatever you bind on earth will be bound in heaven, and whatever you loose on earth will be loosed in heaven." Then he ordered his disciples not to tell anyone that he was the Messiah.
Matthew 16:13-20

Standing near this place called "gates of hell," Jesus began to ask the disciples what the word around town about Him was. *What were people saying? Who did they know Him to be?*

The disciples started by listing off some pretty impressive names: John the Baptist, Elijah, and Jeremiah among others. These were well revered and respected people from the Jewish perspective.

But Jesus wasn't interested in their take on His popularity, so He asked them a second question. Jesus looked at His disciples and asked, *"But who do you say that I am?"*

Peter, in a remarkable moment, responded by saying that he knew Jesus to be "the Messiah, the Son of the living God."

This was a powerful moment because this was the first time that one of Jesus's disciples made a proclamation about the fullness of who Jesus was. Jesus wasn't just a prophet, a rabbi, or a good teacher. *He was the Messiah.*

It's wild to think that just like you and me, these men had grown up in the church culture of their day. They went to the synagogue week after week, they knew the rules, they knew the stories of the greats like David, Elijah, and Abraham. They knew the Torah, and they knew what they were supposed to do to honor God.

But then their teacher Jesus took them outside of their comfort zone to Caesarea Philippi, because there was still *a lotttt* more for them to know. He used this moment to bring a little bit more color to their understanding of who He was, who they were, and what He was ultimately calling them to.

1. Know Jesus.

My guess is that Jesus's questions for the disciples weren't by accident. You see, Jesus was like a celebrity in Galilee at this point. Droves of crowds were coming to see Him, people were attracted by stories of healings and miracles, and with the exception of the religious elite, Galileans thought highly of Jesus and wanted to get close to Him.

But when it came to the twelve men whom Jesus had called to come and follow Him, He wanted more than their admiration— He wanted their *allegiance.*

You see, there is a difference in thinking that Jesus was a *good man* and knowing that He was *God's man* sent to redeem them.

That's why Simon Peter's proclamation was so powerful and why Jesus responded by saying, "Blessed are you, Simon son of Jonah, for this was not revealed to you by flesh and blood, but by my Father in heaven."

I want to pause here and simply ask: *Do you know Jesus?*

If we don't know the fullness of who Jesus is, then nothing else matters.

I don't want to know your church résumé, I don't want to know your Bible reading routine, I don't care to hear about how you manage your sin—I want to know if you've *laid your life down* in total surrender to the one who has the power to redeem your brokenness, renew your identity, and release you to bring the lost home.

Knowing Jesus is about so much more than liking Him or even loving Him! It's about surrendering to Him. When we know the fullness of who Jesus is, we can't help but lay our lives down for His kingdom here on earth.

2. Know who you are in Jesus.

Right after Simon's confession of who Jesus was, Jesus turned right around and confessed who Simon was. He straight up renamed him by saying, "And I tell you that you are Peter, and on this rock I will build my church."

Isn't it cool to think that we don't just *know Jesus*, we are also *known by Jesus*? Jesus knows you, sees you, and loves you more than anybody on this planet even has capacity to fathom.

It's interesting because in the Jewish culture in Jesus's day and age, young boys would attend synagogue for school and training from the rabbi. It was their form of what public school is for us today. Around the age of twelve, they would start separating the good students from the mediocre ones. The elite students would continue their Jewish education, and the subpar students would enter into their families' trades.

When Jesus met all of the disciples, not a single one of them was a part of the religious elite. They were fishermen, tradesmen, and tax collectors. They had been rejected by the religious order of the day and were almost seen as second-class citizens in the kingdom of God.

But there in Caesarea Philippi, Jesus made it known that He was going to do extraordinary things with their ordinary lives. They weren't going to be in the backseat of the Kingdom work anymore. Instead He threw them the keys and declared, *"Now you're going to drive!"*

He looked at the newly named Peter and proclaimed: *"Now that you see me clearly, know that I trust you, and God trusts you to advance His mission. YOU have purpose in My kingdom!"*

My guess is that many of you reading this book often feel like second-class citizens in the kingdom of God. Like you'll never have what it takes to be up there with the pastors, the Christian influencers, and the girls on Instagram who seem to never mess up. But I believe that Jesus wants to rename you as His and He wants to rewrite those lies you've been believing by reclaiming your purpose in His kingdom.

When we truly know Jesus, He begins to show us the fullness of who we are in Him.

3. Make Jesus known.

That's why it's so cool when Jesus told Peter that He was going to use that exact moment, Simon Peter's proclamation, to build His unstoppable church. Jesus isn't building His church on people who always get it right, on the size of someone's following, or on the perfect spiritual experiences. He is building His church on His people's proclamation of knowing who He is.

You see, when you know Jesus, you know yourself and your mission becomes to make Him known to those that don't yet know Him. That's the church! A body of people aiming to know the fullness of who Jesus is, surrendering to being shaped and molded by the character of Jesus, and saying yes to telling everyone about the saving power of who He is.

Jesus says our ordinary lives make up the foundation on which He is going to build His church and the gates of hell will not overcome it. Remember where the disciples were in this story? They were standing a stone's throw away from what the people of that day and age considered to be the physical hell on earth.

Jesus brought them right in front of it and said, *"THIS is where I will build my church, and you—everyday ordinary people—are the ones I'm going to use to do it, and nothing, not even hell itself, will stop MY church."*

I am so excited that we get to spend the next ten weeks together learning how to:

1) Know Jesus
2) Know who we are in Jesus
3) Make Jesus known.

I believe that this book will give you a "back to the basics" moment that we all need, no matter where you are on your journey with Jesus. Whether you've been a Christian your whole life, you've drifted from your faith, or this is the first Bible study you've ever been a part of—get ready to know Jesus like you've never known Him before.

Let's do this together, Delight fam!

XOXO,
Mac Wilson
DELIGHT CO-FOUNDER

PART ONE

Know Jesus

Welcome to section one of KNOWN: Know Jesus.

"I am the good shepherd. I know my sheep and my sheep know me."
John 10:14

Just like Jesus said in John 10, if we are to truly belong to Him, fully living our lives as His devoted daughters, we need to *know* Him. That's what this first section of our Known adventure is all about: getting to know our Savior. Think about it like a friendship! You don't call someone your best friend after one late-night McDonald's run. No, that kind of friendship takes time. You spend time with them, get to know them, get vulnerable with them, then a deep and committed friendship grows from those roots you watered.

Jesus wants to be your friend. This is a great place to start.

The Father's House

WEEK ONE - LUKE 2:41-52

THIS WEEK, WE WILL LEARN HOW TO KNOW JESUS BY MAKING HIS HOME BASE OUR HOME BASE. WE MUST ALWAYS RETURN TO THE FATHER'S HOUSE!

WOW! Can you believe we're here? It's Week 1 of the incredible journey the Lord has planned for us this semester as we dive into *Known.* This past year was ROUGH; a pandemic flipped the world upside down, many of us struggled to see God's goodness, and it sometimes felt like joy was buried by persistent loss. As we begin to see the light appear at the end of this long tunnel, we're excited to start a new journey with you through the Gospels, looking to crucial moments from the life of Jesus.

For Week 1, we're kicking things off with a story from Luke 2:41-52 that describes a moment from Jesus's childhood. It may only contain eleven verses, but there are plenty of awesome details jammed in that we'll comb through together. Buckle up, you're about to be blown away by the goodness of the Father!

Open your Bible to the book of Luke. You'll find it squished between the book of Mark and the book of John. Together with the book of Matthew, they make up the gospels in the New Testament—four accounts telling the story of Jesus's life and ministry on earth. Each gospel has a certain flavor to it based on the author, and Luke is our resident physician. He's got a classic Type A personality: highly detail-oriented and obsessed with laying out all the facts. We love how his personality comes out as he tells Jesus's story. He makes sure not to leave anything out!

Thanks to the author's careful attention to detail, the book of Luke gives us a unique story that is not mentioned in *any* of the other gospels: the story of the boy Jesus at the temple.

Now before you ask, let's dive into why this is unique. You probably know the story of Jesus's birth (if not, it's recorded in both Matthew and Luke). We remember the angel appearing to the virgin Mary and telling her she was going to give birth to the Savior. Then BOOM, nine months later, miracle baby Jesus was born in a stable on Christmas day. BUT, most stories after that are about grown man Jesus. We can take a pretty solid guess that Jesus wasn't born six feet tall with a beard (ew, did NOT need that mental image), so what was He up to during that huge chunk of adolescence? Luke must have been curious about it too, so he gives us this story of twelve-year-old Jesus.

How cool is that? Now that you're on the edge of your seat to learn about middle school Jesus, let's dive in!

Read Luke 2:41-52.

In this story, Jesus and His parents traveled to Jerusalem for the Feast of the Passover. This was not your average family road trip, as they were likely *walking* all the way from Nazareth to Jerusalem. Just in case you're a little rusty on your ancient Holy Land geography, that's about a four-day walk. Now, based on our own experiences of family vacays, we can easily imagine tensions might have been running high as they rolled up to Jerusalem sweaty, dirty, and tired.

Fill in the blanks from Luke 2:43 on the following page.

"After the festival was over, while his parents
were _____, *the boy Jesus* _____
_____ *in Jerusalem, but they were* _____ *of*
it."
Luke 2:43

Mary and Joseph packed up and left Jerusalem to return home,
but young Jesus remained in the temple. His parents probably
assumed He was walking with His cousins or maybe riding His
uncle's donkey, so they kept traveling for a whole *day*. (Yikes!)
Needless to say, as soon as they realized Jesus was missing, they
turned around and headed back to Jerusalem.

After returning to Jerusalem and searching for Him for *three
whole days,* they finally found Him in the temple listening to the
teachers and asking questions.

Put yourself
in Mary and
Joseph's shoes
for a moment.
You are
frantic. Your
firstborn son,

Side Note:

Symbolism alert! God uses three-day periods throughout
Scripture to point toward Jesus and His victory on the cross!

whom you know to be chosen by God as the Messiah, has gone
MISSING. We can imagine the sense of guilt and the burden of
fear that must have been so heavy on their hearts. But think a
little harder—why did it take them three days to find Jesus? Why
did they run from place to place, searching everywhere for Him?
Shouldn't the temple have been the first place they looked?

Are you seeing yourself in this story yet? Sure, we all want to be
like Jesus, sitting contentedly in the Father's house, focused
and engaged not just in the teaching, but also with His Father.

We all want to be like that. But more often we're like Mary and Joseph, trying to find Jesus in all the wrong places, allowing our frustration to rise and our hearts to wander, when He was where we knew He would be all along.

How often do you look for hope, peace, or security in all the wrong places? What is keeping you from returning to the Father's house?

_____

_____

_____

_____

_____

_____

_____

Read Luke 2:41-48.

What word does Luke use to describe Mary and Joseph's reaction to finding Jesus in the temple?

They were **astonished.** Other translations say they were "amazed" or that they "didn't know what to think." We can only imagine the war that must have been raging in their minds. On one hand, they were upset that their son wasn't with them, but on the other hand, they knew that Jesus was something special. What were they thinking? Did they see this as the start of something impossible? The beginning of the miracle of Jesus?

They asked the question on everyone's mind:

"Son, why have you treated us like this?" (v. 48)

We love Jesus's simple response to their anxieties.

"Why were you searching for me?" he asked. "Didn't you know I had to be in my Father's house?" (v. 49)

At first the answer to Jesus's question may seem obvious. Of course Mary and Joseph were looking for Him, He was their son, not to mention a child lost in a big city. But let's take a deeper look.

He said it like it was a done deal. Of *course* He would be in His Father's house. It's not condescending. It's patient and loving. He knew His parents' hearts (perks of being God). He wanted them to understand why He needed to sit there, day after day, even when everyone else left to go back to their real lives. This question gave them a chance to embrace the obvious—Jesus would *always* choose His Father.

But—spoiler alert—the next verse tells us that Mary and Joseph didn't quite understand. *(We can relate to being slow on the uptake sometimes.)*

Read verse 49 again. It can also be translated into "I must be about my Father's work." We love this translation because Jesus wasn't just in the Father's house, He was also doing the Father's work. You see, being in the Father's house and doing His work go hand in hand. Jesus's obedience to the Father shows that His relationship with God took precedence over everything else, even His own family. Even at such a young age, Jesus showed a great love and desire for His Father. Man, don't you want to be more like that?

To wrap this up, copy down verses 51 and 52 below.

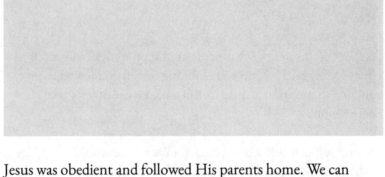

Jesus was obedient and followed His parents home. We can imagine Him turning around as they left the city, taking one last glance at the temple, where the presence of God rested. He allowed His parents to take Him back to Nazareth. He knew He would be back.

Jesus desires you to know His Father like He does. He desires you to be intimate with His Father, to know the depths of His heart. The life of Jesus we read about in the Bible gives us perfect examples of how to fall in love with knowing Him. When life gets hard, know that the Father is waiting for you with open arms to return to His house and fall more deeply in love with Him. He wants you to yearn to be with Him and to be desperate for a chance to sit at His feet.

It's never too late to start. Sit at the feet of your good Father, listen, and be transformed.

Kaylie's Story

KAYLIE PETERSON IS THE TEAM DIRECTOR FOR HER DELIGHT CHAPTER AT TEXAS TECH UNIVERSITY IN LUBBOCK, TEXAS. SHE'S YOUR DREAM HOSTESS, AN OUTSTANDING BAKER, AND A PASSIONATE TYPE 2 ON THE ENNEAGRAM. KAYLIE IS YOUR GO-TO GIRL FOR FASHIONABLE BUSINESS CASUAL ATTIRE AND SHE IS GOING TO BE AN AMAZING TEACHER SOMEDAY.

I have always been a joyful person. I have always been the person to find the good in the bad, and I didn't do it to put on a show. I just truly believed that you can always find good even when life is hard. If you asked all my friends, I'm sure they would say the same thing. Ever since I was little I've been like this. I smiled so much my cheeks would hurt, or I would laugh until I couldn't breathe. That was me all the time. If you go back and look at photos from when I was a child, I was most likely smiling. I loved being happy and I loved being known as that joyful person.

At the end of my sophomore year, the world was struck by a pandemic. Everything was closed, my mission trip was cancelled, and everything just...fell apart. I had a hard time finding joy in my favorite things like hanging out with my friends or even reading my Bible.

Even though I've always been a morning person—waking up at 4:00 a.m. just to enjoy the silence and peace of the morning—it became harder to get up each day. I would lay in bed until I had to be somewhere. I just thought I was in a funk, and I figured I would be fine at the end of the summer. But the summer came and went, the fall semester started, and I was still in a funk. I was sad, unmotivated, and honestly exhausted with life. It got worse as the semester continued, but I pushed it as far away as I could. I was fine—or at least I thought I was.

The hole I found myself in kept getting darker and it was harder to find my way out. I was depressed, anxious, and scared. It got to a point where I knew that I was truly struggling, so I finally told my roommates. I wish I could tell you that was when everything got better, that finally saying it out loud catapulted me into freedom. But it didn't. I continued on with my life for the next three months battling constant unhappiness. I wrote in my journal on November 2, 2020: *I am exhausted mentally, physically, and emotionally. I am tired of trying, I am tired of not being enough, and I am tired of my depression and anxiety.*

Then I did something I hadn't done in months.

I talked to Jesus.

1. The Father's house has to be your home base.

During this time of prayer, I dove into the depths of my brokenness. This was one of the first times I had talked to Jesus about how I was actually feeling, instead of giving Him the sugarcoated version. He revealed three things that changed everything for me:

1. It is not weak to ask for help.
2. Stop trying to do everything by yourself.
3. You have to enter into a crucifixion before you can enter into a resurrection.

While those might seem quite obvious, it wasn't until Jesus told me Himself that I comprehended it. Before this time of prayer, I refused to truly acknowledge my brokenness.

Honestly, I was lost. Like Mary and Joseph, I had been searching everywhere for answers except at the feet of Jesus. I tried pushing it down, ignoring it, and even asking my friends before I finally sought the Lord like I should have been doing all along. I needed to rest in Him, to be transformed and renewed.

Only when I encountered Jesus could I encounter the reality of myself. The reality of myself was that I was depressed, anxious, and desperately looking for healing in all the wrong places. It took me from June until December to truly accept the fact that I needed help—and that needing help was okay.

I went home for Christmas break and scheduled a doctor's appointment. Too scared to say it was for depression and anxiety, I scheduled it for my hip instead. But once I got to the appointment, I finally did it—I told the doctor everything that had been going on, and she officially diagnosed me with general anxiety disorder and depression. Finally having a diagnosis helped me on the way to healing, and it would never have happened if I hadn't asked the Lord for His help. The doctor prescribed antidepressants to combat my symptoms. I remember leaving the appointment and calling one of my best friends to tell her about the prescription because I was so overjoyed that I actually asked for help! I got in my car and cried, ecstatic and proud that I DID THAT! In order for me to get the help I needed and grasp that reality, I needed to return to home base. I had to return home before I could move forward. I had to come to Jesus.

If you don't know where to begin, start with Jesus.

There's a common phrase among Christians that goes, "Jesus is always the answer." Now imagine that as your reality. Ninety-nine percent of the time when we feel confused, lost, or struggling in sin, there's one place we can safely return: to Jesus. Don't know what to do about a boy? Return to Jesus. Don't know if you should take the job? Return to Jesus. Don't know why you keep getting stuck in the same sin? Return to Jesus. No matter what you face, you can always return to Jesus.

But how do we practically do this? Let's talk about actual ways to get back to home base.

+ **Read.** Open your Bible! Daily time in His Word is the best, most foolproof way to hear from the Lord and to sit at His feet. He gave you His Word as a gift and a guide. Use it!

+ **Pray.** Prayer is easier than you think! It's just having a conversation with God. It may feel weird at first, but the more comfortable you are with praising Him and pouring your heart out to Him, the deeper your prayer life will go.

+ **Gather.** Spend time with trusted sisters in Christ! The Lord loves to use the people around you to bring you closer to Him. Try sharing with the other Delight girls! You might be surprised by the benefit of a Christ-centered community.

+ **Listen.** Put on some worship music and try to quiet your mind. It's hard to hear from God if you're always running 100 mph. Take some time to be still and see how the Lord shows up. Don't be discouraged if you don't hear a voice from the sky! Our God works in mysterious ways. Maybe the stillness will just be stillness, but He can still be moving in your heart in the quiet.

2. Your Father already knows your heart.

One of the hardest concepts for me to grasp during this time was the idea that you can have depression and anxiety and still have a relationship with Jesus. I cannot even tell you the amount of times I felt I couldn't go to the Father during this season because

I thought I wasn't good enough. Instead I sat in a pit of darkness. I remember telling a close friend after a really hard night, "I desire to be seen, known, and loved, is that too much to ask?" She said, "The desire you have is valid, but you're seeking it in places that will never fulfill you. Have you gone to the Father?" I remember feeling like someone punched me in the stomach, because the reality was that I hadn't gone to the Father in several weeks, maybe even months.

I had convinced myself that I had to clean up all my mess before I could encounter God—but I promise you that is *not* what Jesus wants. Who are we to assume the Father does not know us?! He formed us in the womb, shaped us into who we are today, and sent His Son to die on the cross for our sins...and we think that He doesn't already know our hearts? We think we have to put ourselves together with a little bow on top? Guess what?! The Father already knows! He knows your brokenness. He knows your sins. He knows your struggles. **Depression and anxiety do not cancel out Jesus.** That's the beauty of the Father. You don't need to be all cleaned up to run to Him.

He wants to encounter us in our brokenness and our mess because He is the only one who truly knows our hearts. He is the one that takes your hand and walks you along the path to freedom, comforting you as you encounter the hurt and pain that result from living in a sinful and broken world. When you feel alone, broken, and sad, run to Jesus and allow Him to encounter the depths of your broken, beautiful heart. He wants to make you new. You can come to Him with anything. I can promise you He understands.

3. You can always come back to His feet.

The only way I could explain to people who didn't have depression what it was like was by saying: "I don't want to live, but I don't want to die." That seems like rock bottom to anyone who doesn't know the hope that a relationship with my God brings. I searched for my purpose and fulfillment in all of the wrong places—on social media by seeking a certain amount of likes on my newest post; through the people around me by being a people pleaser, looking at others for validation and hope; through myself by simply thinking I didn't need anyone else to help me through a difficult time because too many people had let me down and couldn't understand. I was seeking and seeking, but I kept coming up empty. I didn't realize why until one day when I was reading my favorite prayer and was struck by this section:

Keep experiencing the satisfaction that I am.
Keep listening and learning the things that I tell you.
You just wait. That's all.
Don't be anxious. Don't worry.
Or you'll miss what I want to show you.
"Be Satisfied With Me" attributed to St. Anthony of Padua

I have read this prayer over 200 times—I know it front to back. But this line struck me to the core. I realized that I was not experiencing the satisfaction that He offers. I was seeking satisfaction in worldly things, and I wasn't being satisfied. "You just wait," He said. But I was doing the complete opposite of that! Instead of sitting with Jesus through my depression and seeing what Jesus wanted to teach me, I was rushing through it, desperate to get to the end. But the end wasn't the important part.

We will never experience true and total healing and freedom on this side of heaven. That's a fact of the Christian life. So trying to rush through a more difficult season just to get to the other side is like trying to limit God. He wants to use the hard parts of life to grow us, and that can't happen if we're like frantic parents, running all around town for the answers we know only lie at the feet of our good Father. We're just like Mary and Joseph, searching for hope in all the wrong places until we finally find it where we knew it would be: in the Father's house. When you have a relationship with Jesus, you're never too far gone. He found me in my worst moments and showed me how to return to Him. He can do it for you, too.

Conversation Starters

+ How did this week help you know Jesus in a new way?

_____

_____

_____

_____

_____

_____

_____

+ How often do you spend time with God (a.k.a. return to the Father's house)? Why did you choose that answer?

|———————+———————+———————+———————|

NEVER   SOMETIMES   OFF AND ON   PRETTY   I NEVER
REGULARLY   MISS A DAY

_____

_____

_____

+ What have you been running to instead of your Father?

_____

_____

_____

_____

_____

_____

+ How might God be calling you to come back to His feet?

_____

_____

_____

_____

_____

_____

_____

"If you don't know where to begin, start with Jesus."

Notes

The Shepherd's Voice

WEEK TWO - JOHN 10:1-18

THIS WEEK WE WILL LEARN HOW TO KNOW JESUS INTIMATELY BY FORMING A RELATIONSHIP WITH HIM AND LISTENING TO HIS VOICE!

Here we are! Week 2 of Known! If you're new to this whole Jesus thing or brand new to Delight, we hope that this book has already been a game changer for your faith. We are praying for deep conversations, lifelong friendships, and new life with your Savior!

This week we're going to dive into what it means to have such an intimate relationship with Jesus that you know His voice, an intimacy we're going to read about in John 10 through the metaphor of sheep and their shepherd. Fair warning—this week has a lot of analogies, imagery, and figures of speech, so it's going to require some focus! But we'll break it down together, step by step.

Read John 10:1-2.

Who does Jesus address in verse 1?

Okay, our years of grade-school English paid off! We have correctly identified the intended audience of Jesus's teaching here. He was addressing the Pharisees.

What is a Pharisee? Well, we like to think of them as the typical "Karens" of Jesus's day. They were a group of religious leaders in the Jewish community. (If you didn't know, Jesus was actually Jewish!) They were well known for their religious piety, priding themselves on following all the rules laid out for the Jewish people—key word *pride*. These guys thought they were the bee's knees and spent most of their time condemning others whom they viewed as less-than. Based on what we know of our Savior Jesus, these Pharisees were pretty opposite in character from Him, which means they were bound to experience some friction once in a while. This passage describes one of those moments— the Karens had been getting all up in Jesus's grill, so He took a second to set them straight.

This section is confusing right from the get-go. Jesus was talking about...sheep. What?! Before we even start, let's get our imagery and symbolism down. *(Feeling like you're in English class? Don't worry, it gets better!)*

The sheep: You and me! The people God created are referred to as sheep often throughout the Bible, especially in the New Testament. It's perhaps not the most flattering comparison since sheep are pretty dumb and smelly, but you gotta think of the audience. In this biblical context, sheep were super common and much more relevant than they are today. It was an analogy that would connect with everyone.

The sheep pen: Heaven! The kingdom of God! That final destination that we need salvation to reach.

The gatekeeper: God the Father! Our creator who reigns over heaven and earth!

The gate: Jesus! We will get to this later on in the passage.

The shepherd: Also Jesus. Don't worry, it will make sense.

Alrighty. Now that you're an expert on biblical imagery, let's jump into the passage.

In John 10, Jesus starts off by saying that there is only one way to enter the sheep pen (heaven!), and that's through the gate (Jesus). It's a reminder to us that there is only one way to get to heaven. There are no shortcuts.

"...anyone who does not enter the sheep pen by the gate, but climbs in by some other way, is a thief and a robber."
John 10:1

The gate to heaven has been opened for us by God (the gatekeeper) because of what Jesus did on the cross for us. Thinking of His Karen-like audience, we can easily gather what Jesus meant by trying to enter "some other way." These Pharisees were knee-deep in the teaching that good works, and following all the rules, was what got you into God's good graces and into heaven. Jesus was being really radical here—He was telling them that trying to get into heaven by your own merit was nothing more than attempted robbery. Hardcore.

Copy down verse 3 in the space below. It's important.

This is our thesis statement for this week. (Oops, another throwback to English class.) Remember, we are the sheep. This verse tells us that our Good Shepherd, Jesus, calls us by name and invites us to be with Him. All we do is listen to His voice and follow.

Has there been a moment in your life where you felt the Lord call you by name into a relationship with Him? If so, what was it like? If not, what has been holding you back?

_____

_____

_____

_____

_____

_____

_____

Stop and read John 10:4-6.

Just as a shepherd calls his sheep by name and leads them out of trouble, so does Jesus. Remember, sheep aren't the sharpest tools in the shed. They depend on their shepherd for everything. They need the guidance of their shepherd. They rely on his voice. Jesus explained that He is a good shepherd; He knows us each by name and will protect us always.

Pay extra attention to this part of verse 4:

"...his sheep follow him because they know his voice."

Jesus is saying that when we know Him, we will know His voice and be willing to follow Him. But just like sheep, if we don't know the voice we are hearing, we will not follow—because the voice belongs to a stranger.

Have you heard that a mom can recognize the cry of her child even in a crowd? She can be standing outside of a daycare room full of babies and pick out the cry that belongs to *her* baby. That's how intimately we are invited to know our Savior. We are called to know what our Savior's voice sounds like. This is especially important because we live in a world where there are a lot of other voices competing for the top spot.

Let's look closely at verse 6:

"Jesus used this as a figure of speech, but the Pharisees did not understand what he was telling them."
John 10:6

Seems like these Pharisees weren't familiar with their Savior's voice.

Read John 10:7-10.

Due to the fact that the Pharisees still did not understand (relatable), Jesus broke down the metaphor even more, emphasizing how important it is for us to have a relationship with Him. Ultimately, He is the only way to salvation because He is the gate to heaven.

Fill in the blanks from John 10:9.

"I am the gate; whoever enters through me _____ ____ _____*. They will come in and go out, and find pasture."*

Wow! Goosebumps! Jesus just told the gathering crowd that He was the way to salvation. He said it like a promise: if you enter through Him, you will be saved.

But just in case they didn't understand the gate comparison, Jesus hit them with another illustration:

"I am the good shepherd. The good shepherd lays down his life for the sheep."
John 10:11

That's it! The big one! Jesus just foreshadowed His rescue mission for us, when He would lay down His life on the cross so that we wouldn't have to endure God's righteous judgement, allowing us to pass through the gates and enter the promised land, a.k.a. HEAVEN. Sure, the thief may come to steal, kill, and destroy (v. 10), but our Good Shepherd offers us green pastures.

I don't know about you, but I'm starting to feel a little bit better about being a sheep.

Take a moment to reflect on what it means to have Jesus caring for you like a good shepherd. Write your thoughts below.

_____

_____

_____

_____

_____

_____

_____

_____

Skip to John 10:14 and read it out loud.

We are called to be sheep that really know our Good Shepherd. Our life gets to be an exciting journey of getting familiar with our Savior, of learning the unique tone and pitch of His voice.

Read John 10:16-18 and take some notes in the space below.

In verse 17, Jesus says:

"The reason my Father loves me is that I lay down my life—only to take it up again."

Now that's the beauty of the gospel! God sent Jesus to die for us while we bring nothing to the table except the sin itself for which Jesus paid the price. There's nothing you can do to mess it up! So girl, stop being so hard on yourself and just focus on having a relationship with Jesus! He is waiting for you to say YES to His call on your life and get to know Him.

Remember the Pharisees we read about earlier in this passage? They were trying *way* too hard to be perfect and to follow all the rules. But Jesus wasn't having it. What's the point of following all the rules if you don't know how to hear the voice of the Good Shepherd? Are you like those Pharisees, trying and trying, but missing the connection? Are you missing His voice?

How cool is it that the creator of the universe wants to have an intimate, intentional, and personal relationship with YOU?! At first that may seem intimidating. You might wonder...*of all people, why would God want to know me*? The truth is that God looked at the world and thought you were so special that the world needed one of *you*. Having a relationship with you brings Him JOY! So stop stressing about being perfect, and instead strive for progress in your walk and relationship with Jesus! Cut out all the unnecessary distractions and tune your brain to hear your Good Shepherd. We promise, your life will change.

Natalia's Story

NATALIA GRACE IS ACTUALLY AN INFLUENCER, NO CAP. SHE IS THE TEAM DIRECTOR FOR THE DELIGHT CHAPTER AT JACKSONVILLE UNIVERSITY, AND IS KNOWN FOR HER BUBBLY PERSONALITY. NATALIA WANTS EVERYBODY TO KNOW ABOUT JESUS, AND USES HER INSTAGRAM AND TIKTOK ACCOUNTS TO SPREAD THE GOSPEL (IN AN AESTHETICALLY PLEASING WAY OF COURSE).

Growing up, I went to church on Sundays when it was convenient, said the same ten-word prayer before meals, was dragged to Sunday school, and was forced to sing in the children's choir against my will. That was my family's understanding of what it meant to be a Christian—so it became mine. Although there was never a season of my life when I didn't believe in God, there were plenty of seasons when I didn't know Him or hear Him.

I can still picture high-school me sitting on the floor at church camp, begging God to reveal Himself to me so I could be like everyone else and feel Him. I was slowly realizing that going to church and just believing in God wasn't enough. I needed more; I needed to have a *relationship* with Jesus. I was done pretending to be a Christian—I wanted to be the real thing. I began to seek Him by opening my Bible, watching Youtube sermons, listening to podcasts, doing anything to get to know more about Him. But after a while, I realized I was searching in all the wrong places. I needed to go to the source: Jesus!

The first time I truly encountered Jesus, I was laying in my bedroom, staring at the ceiling, unable to sleep after a tough week of battling depression and anxiety. The night before, I had attempted to give up as I felt the weight of the world was too much. My mind spun with thoughts on the meaning of life, my purpose and my worth circling in my brain. Thinking that ultimately my life had no purpose and that the weight of depression, anxiety, and doubt were too heavy to carry alone, I realized I needed to turn to Jesus. I remember weeping at 3:00 a.m. because I finally realized that I didn't have to fight my battles alone; that I had the Savior of the world helping me, that God was on my side and loved me so much He sent His one and only son to die for me. I finally realized that what Jesus did on the cross was personal...it was for ME!

To be honest, I still had no clue where to start in this newfound relationship. Maybe that's you too, and that's so okay! Let's break down together what it should look like to have a relationship with Jesus and be in tune with His voice!

1. You can't follow a voice you don't know.

"His sheep follow him because they know his voice."
John 10:4

How can we be expected to follow a voice that we don't know? In order to have a personal relationship with Him, we must put effort in to get to know Him. In order to recognize His voice, we must seek Him. It was no coincidence that when I started to regularly open the Bible, spend time in prayer, and selflessly worship God, His voice became more clear.

The first time I heard God's voice with clarity, I was overwhelmed. I was on a trip in Atlanta for a time of fellowship and worship with some of my friends and I felt the conviction of God telling me to go on a run. He said that I didn't need to be around everyone—that I just needed to be alone with Him. While I am not one of those athletic girls who enjoy running, I skeptically obeyed and put on my workout clothes. I started running and didn't stop until I came across an old man who was blowing leaves out of his driveway. God convicted me that this man was the reason I was there and that I needed to pray for him. Terrified at the thought of walking up to a complete stranger and asking to pray over him, I began to cry out of fear and begged God—that if this was truly His plan—to have the man come up to me. I wanted to obey, but I was scared.

What if the old man was a kidnapper? What if he hurt me?

There was an endless list of doubts in my heart. Just as I was about to talk myself out of it, the old man walked over to me with a water bottle and asked if I needed anything. I asked him, "Sir, do you believe in God?" He replied, "Yes ma'am."

I asked if I could pray over him and as I was praying, God told me that this man was coming home now. By the end of the prayer we had both fallen on the ground, weeping.

This was just the beginning of my journey hearing God's voice, but it began when I stopped focusing on the sound of the world and focused instead on Him.

2. His Word is good.

The voice of God is good. He really does want to give you the best life!

"My sheep listen to my voice; I know them, and they follow me. I give them eternal life, and they

shall never perish; no one will snatch them out of my hand."
John 10:27-28

This verse isn't saying that bad things won't happen—it's saying they won't happen without purpose, and you will never walk through them alone. It was in some of my darkest moments where I drew the closest to God. When a friend passed away, after I had been sexually assaulted, and throughout my battle with depression, my relationship with Jesus flourished. This is a testament to Jeremiah 29:11:

"For I know the plans I have for you," declares the LORD, "plans to prosper you and not to harm you, plans to give you hope and a future."

The Lord will never lead you astray, even when you face battles that aren't part of the plans you had for yourself. His calling on your life is better than anything you could imagine.

Remember how in our passage, Jesus's metaphor included thieves and robbers? Having a Good Shepherd doesn't guarantee that you won't go through the usual sheep struggles. It means that you have a protector and a promised hope for the future.

3. His voice must be the only voice.

This world is loud. Between the busyness of life, other people's opinions, and the lies of the enemy, it can be hard to hear God's voice. I am no stranger to this. I have never been an insecure person, but in the past year of my life as I've grown stronger in my walk with Christ, I have found myself caught up in the busyness of life: completing my dream internship at my local church, helping lead my sorority's Bible study, being the Team Director for my campus's amazing Delight chapter, and doing my schoolwork. I've often found myself pouring into so many people that I forget to be filled up, which has left me feeling doubtful and insecure about my personality, my body, and most of all God's plan for my life.

What I have found is that these doubts and insecurities stem from not being rooted in my identity in Christ. When you start to listen to other people's opinions instead of what God says, you open the door for Satan to come in and mess with you. When I started to believe the hateful comments, the doubts my parents had about whether I should actively pursue ministry, and the lies of the enemy, I started doubting not only my worth but also my place in the Kingdom and God's plan for my life. As I have learned during this season, when these feelings of doubt and insecurity arise, I need to bring them to the source—Jesus— and re-root my identity and worth in Him. Stepping away to spend time in prayer, worship, and the Word is essential for reducing the noise of the world and focusing only on His voice.

When you get to know Jesus, you slowly start to see your life change. Before I met Jesus, I was complete and solely focused on my own agenda and to-do list. Jesus came in and beautifully wrecked the plans I had for myself, for the better. I slowly saw the posture of my heart and the goals of my life start to shift. It resulted in me changing my major, quitting my sport, and surrendering my agenda to Him.

I have learned that I can trust Jesus when He says that He is a *good* shepherd. Learning how to hear His voice has been the greatest adventure of my life, because His Word is good and His guidance is always exactly what I need.

Are you feeling like a lost sheep? Have you been trying to enter the sheep pen some other way? Do you need to hear His voice again?

Take some time to listen and see what happens.

Conversation Starters

+ How did this week help you know Jesus in a new way?

_____

_____

_____

_____

_____

_____

+ How well do you think you know God's voice? Explain why
you chose that answer.

|———————————+———————————+———————————+———————————|

HE CAN   I'VE HEARD   I'M PRETTY   WE'RE   HIS VOICE
TALK?   HIM ONCE   FAMILIAR   GETTING   IS CLEAR!
      OR TWICE   TIGHT!

_____

_____

_____

+ Is there anything in your life right now that might be preventing you from trusting God's voice?

_____

_____

_____

_____

_____

_____

+ Although it might seem scary, what is one new way you want to tune into God's voice this week?

_____

_____

_____

_____

_____

_____

"The voice
of God is
good."

Notes

The Posture of Unity

WEEK THREE - JOHN 7:25 - 8:11

THIS WEEK WE WILL LEARN HOW TO KNOW JESUS AND HIS HEART FOR EMPATHY! JESUS IS CALLING EVERYONE BACK TO HIM IN UNITY!

It's only Week 3 and we have already learned SO MUCH about knowing Jesus. This week we are going over a pretty intense topic, so buckle up! It seems that lately the church has been so divided; we can all feel it, especially this past year. Political agendas, racial injustice, mental illness, the list goes on. If you can name it, there has been some crazy debating about it, both inside and outside of the church.

This week we're going to be looking at a snapshot from Jesus's ministry to see how He responded in a moment of crazy cultural and religious tension. We pray that looking to Jesus in this story will teach us how to choose radical empathy in times of extreme division.

Division isn't anything new to Jesus. In fact, people even fought over who they *thought* Jesus was when He was on this earth! This week we're going to be diving into John 7:25–8:11 where we are introduced to division in the church and the remarkable story of Jesus and the adulterous woman.

If you read our Delight study on the book of Acts, you might remember when we read about John (this week's Gospel writer) going to the temple with Peter and witnessing Peter healing a crippled man. We also went through the book of John together step by step in our "John" Delight devotional! Whether you're an OG member or brand new to Delight, a quick refresher will get us ready for Week 3! We'll go through it together:

John was one of the twelve disciples of Jesus, one of the most prominent leaders of the early church, and believed to be the author of five books of the Bible—John, 1 John, 2 John, 3 John, and Revelation. He was one of the three disciples closest to Jesus (along with Peter and James) and the disciple whom Jesus commissioned at the cross to take care of His mom after His death and resurrection.

Alriiiiight. Now that we're pretty much experts on the Gospel writer John, let's head on over to John 7:25 to begin our journey together!

Read John 7:25-41.

The story starts off with some crazy tension. Have you ever seen middle school fangirls fight over who knows Harry Styles better? That's basically how you could describe the scene—a blown up argument among the Jewish people at the Festival of Tabernacles, who disagreed over who they thought Jesus was. Some were against the teachings of Jesus and some were for the teachings of Jesus, and they were going *at* it with each other. It probably sounded a little something like this:

One side shouted, *"Jesus is NOT the Messiah! We know where he was born!"*

While the other side yelled back, *"Jesus IS the Messiah! He literally raised people from the dead!"*

All the while, Jesus stood in the middle of the feuds, totally chill, and reminded the crowds that He was the Messiah—that God brought Him to earth to save everyone! *(YES, even the people who were so vocal against Jesus at the festival!)*

What an amazing Messiah Jesus was and is! Can you imagine complimenting someone who despised you? Jesus told people who wanted Him convicted that God loved them! What a wonderful example of humility.

Fill in the blanks below from John 7:38.

"Whoever _____ in me, as Scripture has said, _____ of living water will flow _____ _____ _____."

In times of doubt, Jesus provided everyone with security! He promised everyone that God could provide them with eternal life. The word *whoever* in verse 38 is crucial! Jesus's invitation to all people, from the self-righteous Pharisees to the Gentiles, and to the common Jews who found themselves in the temple courts, reminds us of the utter inclusivity of the gospel. Jesus wanted to unify these opposing groups through a relationship with Himself. We saw these people doubt Jesus's authority and plan of redemption, but their doubts didn't negate His invitation to salvation for all. This is true for us as well and we are SO thankful!

Speaking of Jesus welcoming people into His amazing church, let's zoom in on how Jesus personally welcomed and loved one woman that the religious leaders quickly tossed aside in John 8!

Read John 8:1-11.

John 8 starts us off as Jesus left for the Mount of Olives while everyone else went home after fighting over His credibility as the Messiah.

Side Note:

The Mount of Olives is heavily associated with Jesus and is pretty prevalent throughout the Bible! After the ever-so-famous Last Supper, Jesus immediately went to the Garden of Gethsemane—located at the foot of the Mount of Olives—to pray to His Father before being arrested (stay tuned for Week 9 when we go into this story in detail!). Jesus also went to the Mount of Olives on a regular basis with His disciples. He even spent the night there numerous times. Although it isn't clearly stated, we can conclude that the reason why Jesus went to the Mount of Olives was to connect with His Father.

The next morning while Jesus was teaching His followers in front of the temple, the Pharisees interrupted Him (umm...how rude *and* BOLD?!) by bringing in an adulterous woman and demanding Jesus convict her in front of everyone.

Just in case you're reading this passage and are a little confused about what adulteress meant in biblical times, go ahead and copy down John 8:4 in the space below.

Notice how they said that she was *caught in the act.* We don't want to get too graphic here, but we can imagine that this woman was not in her best moment. It's possible they pulled her right out of some man's bed and dragged her out into the street to face judgement. Was she fully clothed? Was she crying? Did the man she was with run and hide? Had she expected him to stay and defend her?

Oof. Anyone else feeling sorry for this woman right about now?!

If we hadn't already figured out that the Pharisees wanted to trap Jesus by putting Him on the spot to convict the adulteress, John says it outright (v. 6). The Pharisees wanted to leverage disobedience to the law against Jesus so they could justify accusing Him. Little did they know that Jesus knew about their plan all along! Instead of joining the crowd to condemn the adulteress, Jesus took a simple step back from the teachers and wrote on the ground with His finger.

Can we just process that for a sec? How many of us reading this have given into peer pressure because we were scared of what others would think if we didn't join in? Let Jesus's ability to dissociate Himself from the pressure of the voices around Him be an inspiration for all of us to take a step back before we act!

Now, look at what He said next.

"Let any one of you who is without sin be the first to throw a stone at her." John 8:7

WOW! Jesus was a straight up G! Now, we know that Jesus is both fully God and fully man, and that God is by nature a *sin killer.* Unrighteousness can never stand in the presence of God. So, don't read this verse and assume that Jesus was saying she didn't do anything wrong. Adultery really was against Jewish law!

The earth-shaking beauty of this line wasn't even for the woman—it was for the people who were clamoring to condemn her.

Jesus was calling them out, shining a light on their hypocrisy. He was *humbling* them, causing them to relate their sins to hers, leading them to *empathy*. Jesus's response here reminds us of a verse from Matthew.

Fill in the blanks from Matthew 7:5 in the space below:

"You _____, first take the plank out of _____ _____ _____, and then you will see clearly to remove the _____ from your brother's eye."

Jesus's message here was pretty clear: you're all on the same level!

Doesn't that line just make you so proud to be a follower of Christ? An adulteress was shamed in the presence of Jesus and instead of condemning her, He stood up for her **in front of everyone who condemned her.** He stood up for her *even though* she was still in the trenches of her sin! If you're scared to confess to Jesus about a certain sin that you're going through, take note of the way Jesus stood up for the adulteress instead of shaming her for sinning. By addressing the crowd, He called everyone there that day to take on a humble heart posture. When we submit ourselves to a posture of humility, we can finally understand where others are coming from.

That's the first step to empathizing like Jesus.

Have you ever been in a situation where your friend told you something they did that was

unholy? What was your immediate reaction and why?

_____

_____

_____

_____

_____

If you condemned them, what are ways you could have shown them love instead of judgement?

_____

_____

_____

_____

_____

This story would not be complete without the ending.

Read John 8:8-11.

Go and sin no more.

Jesus was not just going to leave this woman in her brokenness. He was on a mission to offer her HOPE. Sure, He led with empathy, but that empathy was a miraculous *tool* for His greater purpose.

Whether you have ever recognized it or not, Jesus has shown you that same empathy and grace in your own life. He's probably shown it to you countless times. So the question is: have you allowed that empathy to change you? Have you put down your stone and walked away, like the men in the crowd that day?

And you know what else? He offers that grace to *everyone,* not just the people who look like you or the people who look like they have their lives together. He offers it to your mean neighbor, the sassy barista at Starbucks, and your childhood bully. We have a Savior who stood in the face of division and inspired unity while still holding on to what He knew to be true. Those men in the crowd were right in their understanding of the law, but they were still wrong. Their hearts were out of alignment because they were missing the character of Jesus. This week, we get to learn from His example.

We get to look a little bit more like Him.

Elysia's Story

ELYSIA WILLIAMS IS YOUR NEW BEST FRIEND. SHE'S AN ENGLISH MAJOR WITH A MINOR IN CREATIVE WRITING AT CALIFORNIA LUTHERAN UNIVERSITY WHERE SHE SERVES HER DELIGHT CHAPTER AS TREASURER (PRETTY AND SMART, THE WHOLE PACKAGE). SIA REVISITS HER ONE DIRECTION PHASE EVERY COUPLE OF MONTHS AND HONESTLY, WE CAN'T BLAME HER.

Hello friends! My name is Elysia but most people call me Sia (like the singer). This is my story about the importance of unity in Christian communities!

Summer 2020 was difficult for all of us, but particularly for my people, the Black community. I want to share with you one of my experiences as a Black woman, but to be honest, I could write a whole novel about the heartbreaking experiences I've endured because of my race. I'm sure a lot of Black women feel the same as I do or have experienced something similar to what I'm about to share—so my prayer is that sharing my story encourages you to speak up about your own experiences to your chapter, friends, peers, and family in order to promote unity!

Even though I danced on and off my whole life, it was in my freshman year of high school when I discovered my love for dance. I was still figuring out my identity, my interests at school, and how I fit into my friend groups, but I knew dance was the one thing I could rely on. I loved the way my body expressed feelings that I couldn't voice and told a story.

However, I was still self-conscious about the way I expressed myself since I struggled with my confidence. One day in the dance studio at my school, a bunch of girls were talking about trending dances—YES, this was the year of the Nae Nae and hit the Quan *(if you know, you know)*. All of us did the dances and were having fun, until someone saw me dancing and yelled, "Oh my God, you are the whitest Black girl I have *ever* seen!"

Those words turned my laughter, joy, and contentment into shame, insecurity, and uncertainty. My insecurities only got worse as the girls on my dance team started to make a list of the "Whitest Black Girls at Chaparral" and put me at the top, right in front of my face. I felt completely invisible as girls started to laugh at and mock my dancing. Is that what everyone thought of me? I started to feel self-conscious about the way I talked, dressed, and carried myself after being accused of pretending to be something that I knew I wasn't. But out of all the things I began to analyze, nothing hurt more than starting to hate the one thing I enjoyed—dance.

After our dance team met I ran to the bathroom and called my mom. Tears of frustration, hurt, and embarrassment clouded my eyes. I could barely express how I felt in that moment to my mom, but she knew how I felt because that's how mothers are. She attempted to reassure me that I was one of the best dancers on the team and that I shouldn't let a few jealous girls take away my pride and joy. (*Also, can we take a moment to recognize the unbelievable amount of times I've cried to my mom on the floor? We love Violet!*) But I immediately shut down any words of encouragement. The girls' comments were already engraved in my brain, telling me I wasn't good enough, that I couldn't dance, and that I was disowning my own race.

At lunch I tried expressing the situation to my friends but their only response was, "that sucks," as if I was telling a story about how I scraped my knee. I instantly started to tell myself that it wasn't that big of a deal. Maybe they were just telling the truth. I wish I could say it got better on the dance team and I triumphantly waltzed in the next day embracing myself, but I quit the dance team the following year and convinced myself that I made the right decision. High school was filled with both amazing successes in numerous clubs *and* times of trial that resulted in lifelong lessons, but I still felt a hole in my heart that needed mending. I wanted to feel wholeheartedly accepted and heard—knowing now that I'm an Enneagram Type 4 explains a *lot.*

1. The power of posture.

I wanted friends who could empathize with my struggles even though they couldn't personally relate. That's one of the things I love most from the story of Jesus and the adulterous woman. In a moment of high tension before speaking or addressing the situation at hand, He paused and changed His position. He simply bent down, lowering Himself in a posture of solidarity with the woman. I can imagine that His posture alone spoke volumes to the crowd that day. The Pharisees wanted Jesus to condemn the adulterous woman for her sins, but instead Jesus saw her as human and worthy of being His first. His posture communicated empathy.

Isn't it crazy how powerful posture can be? How it can almost speak louder than words?

The same is true in our conversations surrounding unity. We have to posture ourselves in order to truly *know* people on a deeper level, to try to empathize with their pain like Jesus would before we ever try to speak into their experiences.

I wonder for all of us what it would be like for us to get on the level of those that are hurting because of racial injustice and try to meet them in their pain, hurt, and brokenness. I know that opening up your hearts to conversations about these things can be scary and uncomfortable, but it is so needed. Maybe you've been thinking...

What if I say the wrong thing?
What if I'm misunderstood?
What if I unknowingly hurt someone?

My challenge to you would be to simply posture yourself in a position of trying to empathize and listen first. In my own experience, even my white friends' simple choice to sit with me, listen, and lament on my behalf has meant so much. I so believe that like Jesus, your choice to change your posture toward these conversations and the people whose experiences that are different than your own quite literally has the power to shift the atmosphere around you. It can unleash deeper empathy, healing, and *change.* That's powerful!

I've seen plenty of Christian churches, Instagram influencers, and Christian peers stay silent on the topic of racism simply because they don't know what to say, don't want to get involved, or are afraid to say the wrong thing. However, the one thing that can help solve this problem in our community is the church being more like Jesus.

By looking at how Jesus interacted with the adulteress, we see that Jesus didn't follow the rules of culture and religion—He chose radical empathy first. If your chapter is struggling with what to do when racial injustice arises, I encourage you to *listen.* It is scary, but it's worth it for the Black and brown girls who feel unheard in our Christian community. Unity can happen in your friendships, your communities, and your Delight chapters with a simple posture of humility and empathy.

Writing about my high school experience with racism brings back so many emotions. Even as I sat down and revisited it, tears streamed down my face. I feel sorry for that girl who had no friends to listen to her, empathize with her, and most of all the girl who didn't know how much God cared for her. I wish I could tell her that in college she will find a loving community and friends who listen to her in the presence of the Lord. I wish I could tell her God was always there to listen to her broken heart.

Freshman year of college was a huge turnaround for me. I started to embrace my natural hair and my Blackness, I had the BEST roommates who became my forever friends, and I rededicated myself to Jesus through Delight! One night at a Delight meeting, I was able to share this story with my community. I was surrounded by people who didn't look like me but empathized with me. They postured themselves to try and meet me in my pain! My community reassured me of the power of presence, beauty, and originality. My best friends even wanted to— lovingly—fight those girls for me. (*We love a girl squad!*)

Being embraced with grace, love, and support helped me heal those wounds that I kept inside of me for so long. Their ability to empathize like Jesus was more powerful than words could ever describe, and I don't ever want to take that lightly. Being vulnerable with my Delight sisters, who are now some of my best friends, truly showed me the power of sharing your story with God's community.

2. Unity starts by spotlighting your own heart.

I know that my experience with my Delight chapter may sound like rainbows and butterflies but to be honest I was SO nervous to share my story! I wasn't sure how my community would receive it but I knew I had to be willing to share the depths of my experiences in order to trust and know that all parts of me would be received with love.

I think in order to have these important conversations we must *all* be open to looking at our own hearts and letting Jesus search them thoroughly so all people can feel supported when sharing their story with us.

I love that Jesus's first response when the Pharisees wanted Him to condemn the adulteress was:

"Let any one of you who is without sin be the first to throw a stone at her."
John 8:7

He told everyone to turn the spotlight on their own heart first, and to take a thorough investigation and inventory of their own shortcomings, biases, sins, and flaws before condemning somebody else. In race/unity conversations we have to be willing to do this with Jesus before we ever try to speak our minds. Isn't it true that we're often too quick to condemn the other side before we've looked at our own hearts? Let Jesus take a spotlight to your heart before you cast a stone in this conversation.

I love Psalm 139 and the example it gives us of what it looks like to invite Jesus into to take inventory of our hearts:

"Search me, God, and know my heart; test me and know my anxious thoughts. See if there is any offensive way in me, and lead me in the way everlasting."
Psalm 139:23-24

I want to encourage all my POC (people of color) women in Delight chapters to speak up! I know, I know. Speaking up is *scary*. You're afraid of how others might process your trauma, afraid of the discomfort this may cause, or you're afraid of the outcomes of the conversation. All of these reasons are extremely valid and normal! But remind yourself that you will never know the outcome until you try.

3. The darkness isn't winning.

I love that right after Jesus's interaction with the adulteress, He tells her to go and sin no more. It's almost as if He's encouraging her to not let the darkness from her past enter into the brightness of her future with Him.

I don't think it's any accident that the very next part of John 8 talks about Jesus declaring that He was the Light of the World. Jesus was and STILL IS winning over the darkness of disunity! Do you believe it?!

The power of Jesus in us is the best weapon we have in the fight against the disunity we see everywhere. Matthew 5:14-16 says that through our relationship with Jesus, we are the light of the world too! We get to defeat the darkness with the light of Christ. Sometimes it feels like our world is so dark but Jesus wants to give us the power of His light to go into every sphere and corner of our world and beat down the darkness with the light of unity!

It's crucial to acknowledge that as a Christian community we can't praise together, share testimonies with each other, and develop Christ-centered friendships while ignoring that some of our sisters go through deeply painful experiences due to racial injustice. As a community, we don't get to pick and choose certain parts of a person to understand. We have to fully accept someone in order to love them and live like Jesus! Jesus doesn't pick which parts of us to love, He loves all of us completely. We need to do the same.

4. What can you do?

Unity will only be successful for followers of Christ if we study who Jesus is and lead by His example. Here are three steps to actively promote unity in your chapter!

Empathize

Stoop down and spotlight your own heart to see what you need to fix in order to fully support your sisters. Be open and willing to have conversations with people and to simply listen with radical humility when you cannot understand.

Evangelize

Spread the word about the ability to have a loving relationship with Jesus! He is our hope and security during times of division. It's the power of Jesus in us that has the power to bring about change. The more people who aim to love like Jesus, the more unified we will be!

Create a Space for Conversation

Go into your Delight meeting this week with the intention of having conversations about experiences of racial injustice! Post about it on your Delight Insta feed, story, etc. in order to encourage girls to keep an open mind and open heart for this conversation!

I know this is all hard to process, but we did it together! Knowing who Jesus is gives me hope that He gave us all the tools we need to help our broken world. I hope reading my story gave you hope too!

Conversation Starters

+ How did this week help you know Jesus in a new way?

_____

_____

_____

_____

_____

_____

_____

+ How comfortable are you with hard conversations? Explain why you chose that answer.

|———————+———————+———————+———————|

NOT AT	I AVOID	UGH, IT ALWAYS	ONLY IF I REALLY	BRING 'EM
ALLLLL	THEM WHEN	TURNS INTO A	TRUST WHO I'M	ON!
	I CAN	FIGHT	TALKING TO	

_____

_____

_____

+ Spotlight your heart. Is there any hurt, bias, or unforgiveness that you have been holding on to? Name it here.

_____

_____

_____

_____

_____

_____

+ We believe that the darkness isn't winning when it comes to injustices in our world today! How might God be calling you to be a light in your community?

_____

_____

_____

_____

_____

_____

"We get to defeat the darkness with the light of Christ."

Notes

Notes

PART TWO

Know who you are in Jesus.

Congratulations! You have leveled up! We are now on section two of KNOWN: Know Who You Are in Jesus.

"And [you] have put on the new self. You are being renewed in knowledge according to the image of your Creator."
Colossians 3:10 CSB

When we meet Jesus, we are not supposed to stay the same. Encountering Jesus changes us, calling us into more and molding us to be the women that God created us to be. That identity transformation is what we will be exploring in this section. Now that we know Jesus, what does that mean for us? Who does He say we are?

Let's find out!

Keep Asking

WEEK FOUR - LUKE 18 : 1-8

THIS WEEK WE WILL LEARN WHO WE ARE IN JESUS BY REALIZING THAT OUR GOD HEARS OUR PRAYERS! WE CAN COME TO HIM WITH ANYTHING AND HE CALLS US TO PRAY AND NEVER GIVE UP!

Wow! Here we are! Week 4! God is moving so clearly in your Delight chapters already, and our expectations are high for what He will do in this section of our book. Let's allow this momentum to launch us into Week 4 of Known!

We are diving into the book of Luke this week, and WOW are you guys in for quite the story! Now if we know anything about the book of Luke, we know that it's full of parables (which are just really cool stories to illustrate spiritual lessons with great truths!) that Jesus used as He interacted with individuals, small groups of disciples, the large groups of people who followed Him, and even further—you and me!

This week we'll look at the parable of the persistent widow. From afar, we may not have a whole lot in common with the characters in the story, but we can guarantee that God has something special in store for you. As we read this week, let's ask the Lord to give us an open heart, open eyes for what He wants us to see, and for wisdom to understand and apply this incredible lesson to our own lives!

Let's open our Bibles, get in our cozy zones, and flip to Luke 18. This parable is on the short side, so we are going to break it down into tiny pieces!

Pause and read Luke 18:1 for an opener you don't want to skim over!

Fill in the blanks below.

"Then Jesus told his disciples a parable to show them that they should _____ _____ and _____ _____ ____."

Luke tells us that Jesus, as the good teacher He is, made the purpose of this story very clear: always pray and never give up. Maybe prayer is new to you or maybe you have been talking with Him for as long as you can remember. Regardless of what your time with Jesus looks like in this season, He wants you to know that He is with you all the time. He encourages us to ALWAYS pray, but that doesn't mean we always have to be in "prayer position" in order to be in His presence. His Spirit is already within you, so take advantage of that power, sister! He wants you to pray in eager anticipation for Him to move!

"Always pray" seems pretty simple to understand. We have a God who is always listening, *duh*! But, why would Luke add "never give up" in there? Let's dive into this Scripture to find out!

Read Luke 18:2-5.

Here we are introduced to two characters. Write who they are below!

1) _____

2) _____

Let's focus on the widow and her request first! Widows were often used as examples in Scripture to highlight not only their vulnerability, but also their persistence in their faith. This is because of their tough position in society, which was low on the social ladder, and because widows didn't have much hope to scrape together a new life after the loss of their husbands. We read that the widow asked the judge for justice against her opponent. We aren't given all of the details of the argument, or what this person did to her, but given the context we can assume that justice was deserved for her. Maybe someone was taking advantage of her simply because she was a woman and no longer had a husband. Someone could have even come into her home to steal her property. Maybe the person was cutting her short and not giving her a payment she needed. Regardless of the circumstances, someone had wronged her—and she boldly expected the judge to make things right.

Okay, so maybe you aren't relating to this whole helpless widow thing. Picture a five-year-old in kindergarten class—we'll call her Sally. The class bully just stole Sally's toy, so she runs to the teacher to tell him to give it back, but the teacher *totally* ignores her because the bully kid's mom donates a lot of money to the school board every year. Are you mad yet? That little girl deserves justice!

If Sally represents the widow in our Bible story, the mean teacher represents the judge. As we read together, the judge "neither feared God nor cared about people" (v. 2). I don't know about you, but this makes me wonder why he was appointed to begin with! This man was likely in the position for selfish intentions, and only sought to serve himself. We will come back to talk more about this, but keep in mind that this man does not represent God in this scenario! The judge's character is actually in complete opposition to our Father's desires, as we can see in God's Word.

Let's flip to Deuteronomy 27:19.

Fill in the blanks below.

"_____ *is anyone who withholds justice from
the* _____ *, the* _____ *, or the*
_____*."*

Whoa. So the judge was *definitely* not representing God in this story. Got it.

While the widow (our Sally) fervently, desperately went to the judge with the expectation of justice, he continued to turn her away. We can picture her coming in day after day with the same case, bringing in more and more proof to fight for herself and prove her point. She got the other kids to back her up. She had her mom write an angry letter. She pointed directly at the bully kid who *literally had the toy in his hands.*

Ooops. We're getting too far into this kindergarten analogy. Back to the widow.

She likely started to get more confrontational, because we read in verse five that the judge felt more intimidated by her (honestly, can't say I blame her)! Eventually, he got tired of her "bothering" him, so he granted her justice out of selfish convenience and without genuine empathy. He had no desire to do what was right whatsoever, but simply gave her "her way" in order to get peace. Have you ever had your family, your boyfriend, the mean girl at school, or your teacher give you your way or take your side just so they wouldn't have to deal with you talking or asking about it anymore? Of course it may feel slightly relieving, but it would be so much more meaningful if they had been empathetic and genuinely saw the need that you did! This is so different from how the Father treats us—He never tires of hearing from us, and in fact He welcomes it! He not only sees your needs and areas of injustice, He also feels them with you and wants to intervene for you—just as long as you're surrendering it to Him!

Flip back to Luke 18. Pause and read verses 6-8.

So, why did Jesus use the parable of the persistent widow and unjust judge to teach a lesson? This story intentionally points out the ill character of the judge—not to say that the judge reflects the Lord, but to contrast the two, so we can be *even more* expectant of God! If this selfish and stubborn judge would reluctantly show up for the widow, just imagine how our selfless, empathetic, and loving Father will respond to us when we cry out to Him! God is ready and willing to hear the prayers of all of His sons and daughters, and especially those who are suffering unjustly.

Sister, know that HE HEARS YOU! Just as we saw the Father providing in an unexpected way for the widow, He can also provide for you! It might be in an unexpected way, and it might take some persistence like we saw with the unjust judge. Maybe He will highlight a weakness in your life and challenge you to depend on Him to turn it into a strength. Maybe He will use that classmate or coworker you're not too fond of to soften your heart and teach you to give more grace. He could even use a parent who hurt you to show you that both forgiveness *and* redemption is possible through Him.

But, don't miss that verse we talked about at the beginning!

Rewrite Luke 18:1 in the space below.

NEVER. GIVE. UP.

Your prayer may not be answered the first time you pray it. Maybe not even the second, third, or fiftieth. But, if our Jesus says to keep praying, that's what we're going to do.

Our prayer this week is that you continue to pray fervently and expectantly for God to move in your life, as well as the lives around you. As chaotic as the world may feel, nothing separates us from Him! Let us be as persistent as the widow!

Alex's Story

ALEX MEADOR GRADUATED FROM INDIANA UNIVERSITY SOUTHEAST AND SERVED AS THE MIDWEST REGIONAL DIRECTOR FOR DELIGHT. SHE'S YOUR TYPICAL "MOM" FRIEND WHO ENJOYS CRAFTING, COOKING, AND TRYING OUT NEW COFFEE SHOPS. YOU NEED TO CHECK OUT HER SMALL BUSINESS, SEALED WITH A PRAYER! (@SEALEDWITHAPRAYER ON IG. THANK US LATER.)

Have you ever found yourself in a season or circumstance where you just felt completely hopeless? It can almost feel like the fog will never lift, but you are desperate for a way out. Or maybe you have even gotten so used to the fog that you don't even remember what it feels like to see things clearly anymore. But now you've hit the breaking point, where you simply can't rely on yourself anymore. So, you lay it all at His feet, whether or not you fully believe He can redeem things for you.

"God, I need an answer. I'm not seeing how or where You're working in this and I need SOMETHING. Some sense of hope, peace, or Your presence. Show me more of You."

I needed an answer. I was about to start my first year of college and my whole life was flipped around, in a way that was beyond a typical "adjusting to adulthood" phase. My parents had split when I was about to go into middle school. For most kids, this would absolutely wreck them, but things were so bad that I had actually been praying for my mother to divorce him. My dad had completely wrecked my perception of what love looked like and this naturally affected how I grew up, no matter how much my mom fought for me to have the most normal life I could. Although she never made my brother and me feel like a burden, I saw how much she sacrificed and struggled. We were all in pain, and watching my dad move on and start a new family so quickly was another punch in the gut for my brother and me in an already difficult season.

As the years passed, things got a lot better—or so I thought. My dad and I were on good terms, but there were episodes that would come up, the situation would get scary and sometimes even violent, and the cycle would begin again. The older I got, the more I could comprehend what the actual conditions were, and I eventually became numb to the idea of things ever being normal. Flash forward to my first year of college, and that was the last straw. There was a big change in the legal system for my brother and me that would highly affect my mother, so she was wanting to fight for it—just like the widow. She wanted to see justice, and unfortunately my dad took things out on me. He called me completely in a rage while I was at work (I'll spare you the details), and long story short, this turned into almost six years of complete silence between us with an occasional failed "attempt" to fix things. Not only did this mean I was no longer in contact with my dad, but the conflict also cut me off from my five-year-old sister, who completely stole my heart from the time she was born. Needless to say, my heart stayed angry and broken for a long time.

I never stopped asking God for an answer, but I came to the point where I honestly didn't believe He was going to give me one anymore. I didn't believe He wanted to restore my relationship with my dad, and eventually I arrived at a place where I *thought* I was at peace with it all. I didn't cry about how unfair it was anymore, or even cringe at the thought of looking back at how terrible things were, but in reality, I had just become numb and compartmentalized the pain.

I had been praying and asking for the Lord to move in my father's life—to capture his heart, to redeem his soul, and to restore our relationship which had been so badly broken. There were even times when my father would reach out to me and I thought God was answering my prayers, but I would just get burned once again.

1. Our Father is able, willing, and ready to hear our prayers.

Through the story of the persistent widow, Jesus wants to make something very clear to us: always pray and never give up. The persistent widow requested justice with full expectancy and belief that she was going to receive an answer in her favor. She was willing to come to the judge every day ready for rejection, but still believing that it would eventually end in redemption for her.

For me, I stopped praying for my dad's redemption because I was afraid to let him back in. God had put it on my heart that part of that redemption meant restoring our relationship. Every time I let him back into my life before, something would happen again that would hurt me. Usually, it would entail revisiting those things from the past and it would hurt me that he wouldn't truly apologize or even be willing to be sympathetic and see my side of things at all. Like our friend Sally and our persistent widow, I wanted justice. I wanted my dad to see my pain and what I had gone through. Though the widow never got the empathy from the judge she likely desired, she still got her justice. But our Father is not like that judge—and quite frankly, He knows the deepest desires of our hearts. So it should come as no surprise that He had more in store for me than giving me what I had been asking for. But there was work to do in both my dad's heart and my own in the meantime.

If I'm being honest, I think the reason the Lord waited so long to give me an answer was because I wasn't ready for it yet. He had been listening to my prayers all along, and He knew my heart well enough that He wanted to offer what I *needed* before I got what I wanted. I was so hardened, bitter, and numb—quite opposite of the persistent, expectant character of the widow— and He knew I needed healing first.

What have you been fervently praying for or need to start praying for? Take a moment to share with Him, whether it's for the first time or the hundredth time.

_____

_____

_____

_____

_____

_____

2. God moves in unexpected ways.

So in my season of waiting, I got something I never asked for— but desperately needed.

When I asked for the Lord to give me an answer, I prayed for something specific. I knew how hardened my heart was, so I asked God to show me more of Him, and oh how He quite literally did. There was a huge hole in my life that I tried to fill with achievements, busyness, and relationships that turned toxic. I gave my heart to so many things in the hope that I would feel *something* good. I was eventually so far from God that I couldn't even recognize myself anymore. So, He showed me Himself again. When I found myself *begging* for a sense of His presence after a long season of depression in my first year of college, He completely captured my heart.

Growing up, I thought I knew who God was, and though I did, I did not know what it felt like to truly be in relationship with Him as my Father. For the next six years, He not only showed me more of Him, but He also was gracious enough to show me who I was intended to be. He spent so much intentional time building a strong foundation for me so that I knew what love should feel like from a father. More importantly, I grew to truly know God as the dad who would never let me down.

You could say I was quite content with how life was going when I received a call from my father in January 2020. It was my birthday, and I honestly rolled my eyes when I saw his name pop up on my phone. I was at a Delight gathering and totally could have pushed it to voicemail, but something prompted me to answer. To be honest, I can't even remember all that was said, but I do remember hearing the sadness within my dad's voice. He asked if we could meet up for lunch next time he was in town, and I instantly shut down. Last time we tried that, I left the sandwich shop, embarrassingly, in tears.

Over the next year, we stumbled through quite a few different awkward phone conversations. We had the opportunity to share very honestly where our hearts were at, and I told him that although I wanted the best for him and for him to find peace, I had been really hurt and had become very hardened to the idea of us ever being in a healthy father-daughter relationship. I told him if this was something he desired, that trust would really need to be built from the ground up in order for me to let my walls down at all.

3. When praying for the Lord to move, we have to fully surrender AND fully believe.

I was driving on a rainy day to meet with some Delight girls two hours away when something shifted in my spirit. There was nothing happening around me—just Jesus, me, and the sound of rain. I had this overwhelming sensation and tears started welling up in my eyes. Although I didn't hear God audibly, I immediately felt the prompting to call my dad and forgive him. I had previously told him (and myself) that I had forgiven him, but this was different. This was a deep belief that God *wanted* to mend this relationship.

My unbelief was the biggest barrier. And in the midst of that unbelief, God showed me more reason to trust Him as my Father, my Defender, my Redeemer, my Way-Maker, and so on. The more I got to know His character, the more I got to know His heart, the more I got to know His desires for me. I became more like our persistent widow! The more fervently I prayed and the more I spent time with Him, the more my heart aligned with His. So it should come as no surprise that He prompted me to forgive when the time was right!

As we are sitting here together, I want to point out that each one of us might be in a different season or circumstance. You may be in a season of gratitude, thanking Him for all of your blessings; or you may be in a season where it's really hard for you to see Him moving. It can be so easy to give up or lose heart as referenced in the Scripture we read this week. Maybe you haven't gotten the answer you want, or have felt discouraged in the waiting. This often happens when we dim the power that prayer has! Sometimes, when we find ourselves in this season, reflection really helps.

Reflect on a time He has shown up in a BIG or even unexpected way for you. Maybe even a time He realigned your path for a better one. Thank Him for the things that didn't go your way and praise Him for how He moved through that season.

_____

_____

_____

_____

_____

_____

_____

Everything shifted when I believed the Lord wanted *even more* for me. I would have been completely content where He had me, but the Lord graciously showed me He had more to offer. He was just waiting for me to believe He could offer something that big.

I'm not going to sit here and say things have been easy since then. I mean, as I'm writing this it has only been three months since that day I felt forgiveness for my dad! So when I say I am right there in the middle of this story—I truly am! As a matter of fact, I am going to be seeing my little sister this weekend for the first time in five years, something I have actually been fervently praying for, and a big reason why I'm so passionate about women's ministry in the first place! Y'all, there are no coincidences in the Kingdom! I believe this was in His absolute perfect timing, even to the little details of me sharing this detail of redemption with you all.

What I can tell you is this: God will move, but we *must* trust that He can!

Obviously, my story came with lots of hills and valleys and quite the whirlwind in between. With every curveball, I had to remain expectant that He would make a way. We see in Scripture over and over that God uses the most unlikely people to offer healing and restoration. He used the unjust judge to provide justice to the widow. He used Paul as a catalyst to start the early church. He used Ruth as an example of hope in the darkest season. Know that when things are not going the way you planned, He is revealing something bigger He has for you. There may be a lot of pain or sacrifice along the way, and life may simply not seem fair (like for our friend Sally). We are living among a very broken world, but through your experience He wants to be a light to others. He may even plan to use your story to share His redemption plan with others!

I also want to remind you that there is so much purpose and significance in the dreams and visions He has given you for your life. If your life plan has suddenly shifted, know that the seed He planted for you won't go unwatered. The flower may just have a different bloom than you expected! So let me leave you with this:

God is greater than the burdens you are carrying.

Keep praying and don't give up.

Conversation Starters

+ How did this week help you know yourself in a new way?

_____

_____

_____

_____

_____

_____

_____

+ What prayer have you given up on because you haven't received an answer?

_____

_____

_____

_____

_____

_____

+ Think of a time when God answered a prayer in an unexpected way. What does this reveal to you about His character?

_____

_____

_____

_____

_____

_____

+ Alex shared that her unbelief was her biggest barrier. What stands in the way of you fully surrendering your prayers to God?

_____

_____

_____

_____

_____

_____

"Always pray
& never
give up."

04

Notes

His Temptation Strategy

THIS WEEK WE WILL LEARN WHO WE ARE IN JESUS BY FOLLOWING HIS STRATEGY FOR FACING TEMPTATION. HE WAS TEMPTED, SO WE WILL BE TOO, BUT HE TEACHES US HOW TO HANDLE WHATEVER COMES OUR WAY!

Have you ever seen someone wearing a bracelet embroidered with the letters WWJD? If you grew up in church, you might view the bracelet as a sort of Christian rite of passage, like stacking chairs at youth group or getting your first big-kid Bible. In the midst of any decision in your life, big or small, you could glance down at your wrist and think, *What would Jesus do?* But why is this such a powerful thought? Because, as Christians, we are always striving to look a little more like Jesus. That desire comes straight from the Bible!

"Put on the new self, created to be like God in true righteousness and holiness."
Ephesians 4:24

That seems like an impossible goal! How in the world are we supposed to be like God? All the time?! How do I even know what Jesus would do? There isn't a book of the Bible on how to navigate Instagram in 2021! Be honest. Have you ever thought that maybe the Bible is a little outdated? Have you ever wondered if those people in biblical times had it easier because they didn't have to deal with the internet? You're not crazy to wonder that! But, luckily, our God addresses that worry.

Flip to Hebrews 4:15 in your Bible.

Fill in the blanks below.

"For we do not have a high priest who is unable to _____ with our _____, but we have one who has been _____ in every way, just as we are—yet he did not sin."

Does our Jesus really know what we're going through? Turn to Matthew 4 and let's find out.

Read Matthew 4:1-11.

Whoa! Slow down there! Let's back it up a little bit. Matthew 4 transports us to the very beginning of Jesus's ministry on earth. Scripture tells us that Jesus is about 30 years old in this story. (*That's a message in itself! Have you ever felt like God was taking too long to use you? His own son had to wait until He was 30 to start His ministry!*) Right before this moment, Jesus was baptized in the Jordan River by His cousin John— distant cousins maybe, but it's cute to imagine them growing up together! There was a beautiful moment when God megaphoned down from heaven and told the gathering crowd that Jesus was His son and that He was "well pleased" with Him. Precious! This was definitely a mountaintop moment. What happened next?

Fill in the blanks on the next page.

"Then Jesus was _____ _____ _____ _____ into the wilderness to be _____ by the devil."
Matthew 4:1

Led by the Spirit? To be tempted? *Excuse me?* What a contrast! God just told Jesus He was proud of Him and claimed Him as His own then sent Him into no man's land to starve and—oh yeah, by the way—THE LITERAL DEVIL WAS THERE?!

Dig in here! Don't just skip this moment because it doesn't make sense. Maybe you've read that verse that tells us that God will not tempt anyone (James 1:13) and you're feeling a little confused. Let's talk about that!

Although God Himself won't tempt you, that doesn't mean you will never have to stand in the face of temptation. We see here that the Holy Spirit actually *led* Jesus toward the place where He was tempted—so we gotta know that temptation will happen in the Christian life. But maybe temptation can also have a purpose that just might work out for our good and for the good of the Kingdom.

After Jesus was led to the wilderness, Mr. Devil showed up. He saw that Jesus was hungry and hit Him with temptation number one: "If you are the Son of God, tell these stones to become bread." Talk about hitting Him where it hurts! Satan went straight for the physical need that Jesus was experiencing, taunting Him with the idea of fresh, God-made bread. If this was an area that tempted Jesus, it's something we need to zoom in on for ourselves. Our body and our most basic needs, designed by God to remind us that we must rely on Him, can be a source of temptation. Maybe this is you. Maybe you eat too much to numb the pain, or maybe you don't eat enough for a sense of control. Or maybe it's not even food—maybe your physical need for affection drags you into relationships and situations you never thought you'd be in. Maybe your desire for friendship stings so bad that it feels like a hole in your stomach, so you reach for things and people that God hasn't given you.

How do we respond? What *would* Jesus do?

Fill in Jesus's reply in the space below (Matthew 4:4).

Quick! Flip to Deuteronomy 8:3! Sound familiar?

Yes! You guessed it. Jesus is quoting Scripture to the devil! Could it really be that easy? Let's keep reading!

Turn back to Matthew 4 and read verses 5-6.

Write down a short summary of the devil's next temptation in the space below.

At first, this doesn't sound very tempting. "Jesus, jump off this building!" But if we look deeper, we see two very important things happening here. First, the temple pinnacle in the Holy City was a very public place and the drop was crazy high. So, for Jesus to jump off and be rescued by a horde of angels would be a pretty rad spectacle. The temptation here wasn't to jump off a building; this was about *pride.* The devil offered recognition for Jesus. Who could deny that He was the Son of God after seeing that daredevil (pun intended) act? Second, we see here that the devil knew his Scriptures.

"Your enemy the devil prowls around like a roaring lion looking for someone to devour."
1 Peter 5:8

Satan is not messing around! He knows exactly what he is up against and he will stop at nothing to lead you away from God's glorious plan for your life.

How did Jesus respond? Again, He *quoted Scripture* right back at him—specifically, this one comes from Deuteronomy 6:16 if you want to check it out.

The enemy, aptly named here as the Tempter, wasn't done yet. For his big finale, he showed Jesus all of the kingdoms of the world and said he would give them over—if only Jesus would bow down and worship him. If you didn't think the devil was ridiculous before, this one really puts the nail in the coffin. Imagine asking Jesus Christ, Savior of the World, to worship... you?! Silly.

But we do see something crucial here: the devil had something to offer Jesus. When Adam and Eve sinned in the garden of Eden, they signed this world over to the Tempter himself. That is why everything is so broken—because the devil still has his grip on our world. But what did Jesus, the one who crushes the devil under His heel and gives us hope of eternal life, do?

Write down His response in the space below (v. 10).

James 4:7 tells us that when we resist the devil, he will *flee* from us. Just like the devil fled when Jesus stood on the Word of God and ordered him away, we have the same power in our own lives and in our own temptations to tell the devil to leave in the name of Jesus. Have you unlocked that power in your life?

As God's children, we were built to stand in the face of temptation through the power of Jesus that lives inside of us! To us, that seems like a superpower worthy of a Marvel movie. This week, let's dive into unlocking that superpower in your own life!

Maggie's Story

MAGGIE SAWLER IS THE CURRICULUM DEVELOPMENT COORDINATOR FOR DELIGHT MINISTRIES AND AN AVID SLEEPWALKER (YIKES). MAGGIE STARTED HER DELIGHT JOURNEY AT BELMONT UNIVERSITY, THEN HELPED FOUND A CHAPTER AT THE UNIVERSITY OF NORTH TEXAS BEFORE SERVING AS SOUTHWEST REGIONAL DIRECTOR. SHE RECENTLY MOVED TO NASHVILLE, TN WITH HER HUSBAND DYLAN AND HER PUPPY ROSIE.

I waited until I was married to have sex. Go ahead, clap. That's what I wanted, anyway.

I started dating my now-husband Dylan when I was 16. We met in chemistry class our sophomore year of high school (*I know, so cute*). Dylan and I both loved Jesus before we met. In fact, my first test for him before I let him become my boyfriend was inviting him to my youth group to see if he could hang. Obviously, any man of mine would *have* to go to my church.

He pursued me for months. I played hard-to-get like the good Christian girl I was, then on July 11, 2015 he asked me to be his girlfriend by writing it on the side of a Double Chocolatey Chip Frappuccino from Starbucks. If you're thinking this is a Hallmark movie right now, you're not wrong.

Dylan and I never broke up. I knew by eight or nine months into the relationship that he was the one I was going to marry.

The moment I knew stands out clearly in my head: a friend asked me if I thought that Dylan and I would ever break up and I said, "Who would ever break up with Dylan?" It clicked right then—*Oh, I'm going to marry him.*

Looking back, that should have been the first sign that I had not fully given this love over to Jesus. When you ask Dylan why he married me, or how he knew I was the one, he always talks about the hours he spent in prayer, or the ways that the Lord confirmed things for him. I'm sure I prayed about Dylan. I probably prayed about him and for him all the time. But I don't know if I really gave the relationship to Jesus and surrendered it at His feet.

Flash forward three years, and we were getting engaged at 19. We had been through so much by this point—high school graduation, three different colleges, and a chronic illness. Dylan had stood by me through it all. There was no doubt in anyone's mind that he would always stand by me. We were being good with our boundaries—well, good in comparison to what my friends were doing—and I was spending a lot of time comparing my relationship to theirs. *We* were waiting for marriage. *We* had good boundaries. *We* went to church together. Dylan *never* pressured me and our marriage would be *blessed* because of our good behavior.

When I talked to people about why I was waiting until marriage, which I did *way* too often, I told them it was because my parents did. My parents (shoutout to Rich and Lori) started dating in 8th grade and got married when they were 19. Theirs is the quintessential eighties love story, complete with the boombox outside of the window and a puffy-sleeved nineties wedding dress. They're still together all these years later, and they always reminded us kids that if they waited, then we could too. This stuck in my competitive brain like a leech. If my parents could wait until they were married, obviously I had to. I couldn't let them beat me. So, I resisted that specific temptation. But do you see the problem here?

1. Outward appearance is never enough.

I resisted the temptation to do the "sexy time" with my cute boyfriend because I wanted to prove to myself that I *could*. I wanted to have it all in my power and my control. Reading Matthew 4, we see that resisting temptation is an inner, spiritual commitment, not done for the purpose of appearing obedient or an earthly desire for affirmation.

Jesus was all alone out in that wilderness. Nobody would have known if He had given in and allowed the devil to give Him some bread. He could have taken a little bite and nobody would ever have to know that He cheated, just a little bit. But did He? No. He stood firm on God's promises, relying on His word and resisting temptation even when no immediate reward or recognition seemed close at hand. My prideful, worldly attempt to mirror Jesus only went to show that I am broken and desperately in need of a savior.

Think of a time when you did the right thing for the wrong reasons. How might God be calling you to realign your heart with His?

_____

_____

_____

_____

Soon after we got engaged in a fairytale-rooftop-red-carpet proposal, things started to shift. Suddenly, "don't touch me" became my most used phrase. Our almost-too-far moments watching Netflix in a dark room turned into sitting on opposite sides of the couch with the lights on so I could breathe. Something was happening—I started to have panic attacks when he kissed me, I started crying when married women from my church tried to have the sex talk with me in the lobby, and don't even get me *started* on lingerie shopping. With the wedding looming, my biggest stressor wasn't planning an event for 300 of my closest friends or booking the Mexico honeymoon. I was desperately afraid of my own wedding night.

You see, I was pure. And I was proud of it. *I* had resisted. Wasn't I better than the other girls who hadn't waited? Wasn't I in some secret club they could never gain entrance to? But...what would I be after that night? I had held so tightly onto my virgin identity for so long and with such pride, that the thought of losing it made my stomach twist into knots. I wished we could just skip that part and go straight to lying on the beach with strawberry margaritas.

Alas, my mom said that I had to have sex with him on our wedding night. She said that I would regret it if I chickened out or made a big scene about it. So I did it. Or, I guess the right way to phrase that is, *we* did it. And just like that, I wasn't clean anymore.

I was dirty. I could feel it. Our marriage began, and I was mourning the loss of my purity. I dreaded every kiss, wondering if he wanted sex from me. I began to feel like a bad wife. What was I, if I couldn't give my husband that satisfaction? What kind of wife cries after sex? After a while, Dylan stopped initiating. He didn't want to hurt me.

I was in pain. Why was this happening to me? I followed all the rules! Why wasn't I getting my happy ending?

2. You cannot fight temptation on your own.

Let's get one thing straight. The Lord wasn't punishing me. I was in claws of the devil, listening to all the wrong voices, focusing on all the wrong things, and it was slowly poisoning me from the inside out. The Lord was calling my name, reaching out, but I had no desire to start the long crawl.

I thought that I was resisting temptation, but all I was doing was saying no to one temptation and whole-heartedly giving myself over to another. It was sexual sin either way—by taking pride in my purity and my virginity, I was idolizing sex and elevating it above my God. Isn't that just the same as if I had been sleeping with a new guy every weekend? That's what giving in to any temptation really is: *deciding this thing is more important than God.* I was ignoring God's mighty plan for me and holding too tightly to my own. And it was hurting me. Even worse, it was hurting the man that I loved, and the holy union we had entered into.

In those moments, I wish that I had clung to the Word of God like Jesus did. Yes, the Bible says that sex is reserved for marriage and that I shouldn't awaken love before its time. I could quote those verses to you, but so could the devil. So, what is the difference between knowing Scripture and what Jesus did in Matthew 4?

It's your heart.

Jesus clung to the Word of God like a lifeline. He trusted in it, giving total submission to the Lord's guidance because He knew that He had a Good Father who was working for His good and who delighted in giving Him the Kingdom. Do you trust in your Father like that?

List the things that you have been holding too tightly that you need to give to God.

_____

_____

_____

_____

_____

So, where did that leave me? Was I just as doomed as the girls I thought I was better than? Was my marriage ruined because of my pride?

3. Jesus provides the ultimate victory.

I was on the floor at the church that was hosting the 2020 virtual Delight conference. The band was playing "New Wine" by Hillsong Worship.

Where there is new wine
There is new power
There is new freedom
The Kingdom is here
I lay down my old flames
To carry Your new fire today

Jesus held me in that moment and He told me that we were done with this. He told me that I was free. I could put it all down.

I could leave my shame.
I could leave my guilt.
I could leave my pain.
I could leave my fear.

These old flames were nothing compared to the blaze of my Savior's love for me. His mercy is never-ending and His grace washes all traces of my past.

"Let us then approach God's throne of grace with confidence, so that we may receive mercy and find grace to help us in our time of need."
Hebrews 4:16

This freedom is available to anyone who needs it. Maybe sex isn't a temptation for you, or maybe it is and you've given in and given up. Maybe you give in to gossip, bitterness, porn, pride, or jealousy. Whatever it is, our God promises grace *and* mercy. He can make you new in an instant. He can wipe you clean. Even more uncomprehendingly, He can give you the willingness to resist next time your specific flavor of sin comes to call. He can give you the power to stop trying to do it all on your own.

I came home from that conference different. I find that every true encounter with Jesus changes me, even just a little. Sure, I still struggle with the sex stuff. Often, spiritual freedom from a certain sin pattern won't automatically mean everything gets magically fixed right away. It's a process. Sometimes, I'm not in the mood or we go too long between kissy sessions. But it doesn't hold me anymore. Jesus's power overcame.

He can do the same for you. You know that thing that holds you back? The thing you only do when it's dark, quiet, and you're sure no one can see? The thing you have never said out loud?

It's time to bring it to light. Maybe for the first time ever, you need to believe in God's redeeming power for your life. Your temptations cannot stand against the love, grace, and mercy that your Father offers you.

His hand is reaching out. Will you take it?

Conversation Starters

+ How did this week help you know yourself in a new way?

_____

_____

_____

_____

_____

_____

_____

+ Maggie's temptation was taking pride in her purity. What temptation are you currently facing?

_____

_____

_____

_____

_____

_____

+ How have you been trying to fight this temptation on your own?

_____

_____

_____

_____

_____

_____

+ What do you need to do to truly allow Jesus to have the final victory over your area of temptation?

_____

_____

_____

_____

_____

_____

"We were built to stand in the face of temptation through the power of Jesus."

Notes

Share Your Story

WEEK SIX - JOHN 4:1-30

THIS WEEK WE ARE SWITCHING THINGS UP AND GETTING READY FOR AN AWESOME DELIGHT MEETING WHERE YOU'LL HAVE THE OPPORTUNITY TO SHARE YOUR STORY!

Have you ever heard the story of the woman at the well? It's this great story in the Gospel of John where Jesus reveals Himself as the Messiah to a Samaritan woman while she is drawing water at a well. Go take a look at John 4:1-30 if you need a refresher.

We love the implications of this beautiful moment in Scripture. The woman was a Samaritan and Jesus was a Jew, so socially speaking—according to the norms of that time—they shouldn't have even been talking. Powerful! He told her that He was the key to living water, a well that would never dry. He even gave her some deep pro-tips on how to worship God in spirit and truth! (Trust us, this story is *jam* packed with good stuff!)

Our favorite part of Jesus's encounter with the Samaritan woman at the well starts in verse 16:

He told her, "Go, call your husband and come back."

"I have no husband," she replied.

Jesus said to her, "You are right when you say you have no husband. The fact is, you have had five husbands, and the man you now have is not your husband. What you have just said is quite true." John 4:16-18

At first glance, this seems like an awkward moment. This chick has a *complex* history with men, and Jesus just outed her. Yikes.

But when you dig a little deeper, you see that a part of Jesus's character is revealed.

Jesus values vulnerability.

She wasn't technically lying when she told Jesus that she didn't have a husband—He could have just left it there. So why did He push it? Why pursue the subject? And honestly, why did He even bring the whole husband thing up in the first place? He's *God*! Clearly He already knew all the gory details about her love life. What in the world was Jesus getting at?

Jesus was *revealing* her.

Our God is not a surface-level God. He cares about the hidden things, the dark parts we don't share with the strangers we meet at the coffee shop. He cares about lighting up those dark places, creating room for His goodness to step in. In this story, He proved to the Samaritan woman that He *knew* her. His knowledge of her impacted the woman more than anything else He had said.

Then the woman left her water jar, went into town, and told the people, "Come, see a man who

told me everything I ever did. Could this be the
Messiah?"
John 4:28-29

She ran around town, shouting to everyone she could find that this man *knew* her. He knew the deepest, darkest parts of her. She didn't have to hide anymore, and she saw it for what it was.

A miracle.

We serve a God who really, truly *knows* us. There are no secrets you could keep from Him and no place you could run that would be out of His reach. As we see in the story of the woman at the well, He cares about getting those secrets out in the open. In fact, His example proves that openness and vulnerability is actually a key to freedom.

At Delight, we believe in the power of vulnerability. We have witnessed time and time again the impact that sharing your story can have—not only on your own freedom, but on the depth of your community as a whole.

We believe in this so much that we have carved out this week just for that. For Week 6 of Known, we're continuing a beloved tradition in our chapters: Share Your Story.

Share Your Story week is a way to live out our core value of vulnerable community. If this is your first time with a Delight book, or if you're new to the Christian faith, we know this can sound so intimidating!

I'm supposed to spill my darkest secrets to a room full of strangers?!

Don't panic! We promise that this week will be so powerful for your faith walk! It is a little scary at first, but it's worth it. If it's important to Jesus, it's important to us!

Okay, so how do we do it? Here is how it's going to go down!

In your next Delight meeting, you will have the opportunity to share your story with a small group of women. Your chapter will break into smaller groups and each woman will have 10-15 minutes to dive into some of the things that she's been experiencing lately and what God has been teaching her along the way.

Keep in mind, this is *not* simply a testimony night! We love hearing your story about how you came to know Jesus, but this isn't the moment for that—this meeting is your opportunity to share what you are going through right now. Talk about the thing you haven't told anyone about. Talk about the eating disorder you have been struggling with. Talk about the porn addiction you can't let go. Tell your Delight sisters about the doubt you've been having in your faith. Tell them about your parents, your anxiety, or the party you went to the night before.

This is a safe space. Nothing said in a Share Your Story circle will be repeated outside of Delight. Just like Jesus fully *knew* the Samaritan woman, He also fully *loved* her! There is no room for judgement in a circle like this. We are all in need of our Savior!

Finally, you don't have to deal with it all alone. You may find that other girls in your circle are going through the same thing. Maybe the girls in your circle will pray for you. Maybe your brave vulnerability at this meeting will be the key to unlocking your freedom.

Imagine the power of being fully KNOWN by your sisters in Christ. Remember the joy the Samaritan woman felt, telling everyone she could find that someone *finally* knew her? That joy can be yours this week. Don't miss this opportunity.

Who knows? It just might change your life.

Start Preparing:

+ Have you ever shared your story before? What scares you about opening up in this way?

_____

_____

_____

_____

_____

_____

+ What are you currently struggling with? Maybe it's something you're doing behind closed doors, maybe it's a hard situation you're walking through, or maybe it's a moment you've tried to forget? Share it here first.

_____

_____

_____

_____

+ What parts of this story are you most afraid to open up about? What do you think people would think about you if you were really honest and vulnerable about it?

_____

_____

_____

_____

_____

_____

+ What do you think God wants to say to you when it comes to this specific situation?

_____

_____

_____

_____

_____

_____

The Crowded Heart

WEEK SEVEN - MARK 9:30-37

THIS WEEK WE WILL LEARN WHO WE ARE IN JESUS BY MAKING ROOM IN OUR CROWDED HEARTS FOR HIS LOVE. THEN, WE CAN FULLY STEP INTO BEING THE PEOPLE HE CALLED US TO BE!

Welcome to Week 7 of our expedition to *know* our Savior! Hopefully by this point, you're feeling smarter, wiser, and much more equipped to tackle some Scripture than you felt at Week 1. This week, we're taking things *slowwwwww*. We are studying a short, *seven-verse segment*. If you've ever wondered how jam-packed the Bible is with wisdom and teaching, this week will leave you amazed at God's communication skills through His Gospel authors.

For the first time in our Known journey, our story takes place in the book of Mark. The Gospel of Mark is the most succinctly written account of the life of Jesus. This is the shortest and *definitely* the most to-the-point. Mark didn't waste any time getting into the root of Jesus's teachings and the experiences of the disciples. Well, Mark, we appreciate you. Sometimes a girl needs some straightforward teaching!

Go ahead and read Mark 9:30-37.

You may have noticed that there is *a lot* packed into this tiny portion of Scripture! Before you get whiplash, we want to help you out by giving you a little thesis statement for what we are hoping you will learn today:

The disciples' hearts were too crowded by comparison, bitterness, and pride to hear the important message Jesus was trying to tell them. We challenge you to see yourself in this story. What is crowding your heart and what might you be missing out on?

Keep that in the back of your mind as we continue our study! Now, let's dive in!

Your Bible probably labels the heading for this passage something similar to "Jesus Predicts His Death a Second Time." *Yikes.* It seems like a bit of a downer, right? Before you jump to any conclusions about how sad and worried the disciples must have been after their teacher and friend told them He was about to die, look at verse 32 again.

Fill in the blanks from Mark 9:32 below.

"But they _____ _____ _____ what he meant and were _____ to ask him about it."

Yup. So, the disciples were in the dark here about the gloomy prediction Jesus had just made. This is a theme we see a lot in the Gospels. Jesus would often tell His disciples something important and profound, but the author would clarify with something like, "But the disciples did not know what he meant."

We can interpret this reaction in two ways. Sometimes, the Father clouded the disciples' minds and didn't let them understand because it wasn't their time to know yet. Divine timing is a *great* excuse for confusion. The second way is slightly less flattering for the disciples. Sometimes, they didn't understand what Jesus was saying because they were too *distracted* by their own issues.

Sadly, we think the confusion in today's passage stems from the second option, or maybe a little bit of both.

Copy down Mark 9:33 in the space below to see why the disciples may have been distracted.

You got it—the disciples missed an important warning from Jesus because they were *arguing*.

Let's take a second to gather some background for this moment. At the beginning of this passage, we found out that the disciples had just arrived in Capernaum. Capernaum was Jesus's home base at this time, a fishing village located on the northern coast of the Sea of Galilee. It's a place we see popping up all over the Gospels, a place where lots of healings, miracles, and teachings happened.

Okay, so we know the *where,* but what about the *who?* Jesus kept a squad of His close buds with Him during His travels who were called disciples, sometimes referred to as the Twelve. They were a motley crew, a mix of people ranging from fishermen to tax collectors. The one thing that united them was a call from Jesus—each one of them left everything behind to join this rabbi in His ministry. And if you've ever spent a lot of time with one group of people, you know conflict and tension is inevitable. That's what happened here.

In verse 33, Jesus asked the disciples what they were arguing about on the road.

Take a look at verse 34 and fill in the blank below.

"...On the way they had argued about who was the _____."

Mark doesn't specify which disciples were having this argument, but we like to picture Simon Peter and John as the culprits. Peter, a well-known favorite of Jesus's, seemed to enjoy his high-up place in the ranks. We even read about him attempting to *correct* Jesus sometimes. John, hilariously, called himself "the disciple whom Jesus loved" every time he mentioned himself *in his own Gospel*. So, these guys may have had some ego happening, spurring them to have a public argument about who was the best. (Is this feeling like an episode of *The Bachelor* yet?)

On top of all that, we see that after Jesus asked the disciples what they were arguing about, even though He clearly already knew, the disciples *stayed quiet*. Oops. Caught in the act!

Pay attention to Jesus's response in verse 35.

"Sitting down, Jesus called the Twelve and said, 'Anyone who wants to be first must be the very last, and the servant of all.' "
Mark 9:35

We can imagine Peter and John's jaws dropping, shock written all over their faces. Jesus stopped the whole crew to utilize this moment for teaching—like when you're on a road trip and your dad has to stop the car and turn around and look you in the eyes to correct your behavior. Jesus told the listening disciples that being a servant is *most* important of all.

Even more important than being the greatest disciple? What?!

To be the greatest, you have to lower yourself into the position of a humble servant. And in order to embrace humility, you have to check your stubbornness and pride at the door. Man, we are sharing in the conviction that the disciples must have felt at that moment.

Think of a time where you tried so hard to be the best that you found yourself cutting corners and hurting others to get there. How might Jesus be calling you into a servant-hearted posture?

_____

_____

_____

_____

_____

_____

Then, Jesus threw a major curveball and picked up a *little kid* to illustrate His point. He used this child to teach the disciples about humility and His upside-down Kingdom. Jesus said the greatest must also be the least—only in loving others are our actions important.

"Whoever welcomes one of these little children in my name welcomes me; and whoever welcomes me does not welcome me but the one who sent me."
Mark 9:37

Not only is the last the first, but welcoming the least of these means welcoming Jesus and, therefore, His Father. Whoa.

You might be wondering why Jesus used a child to explain His point to the disciples. In this context, children were seen as weak and were considered the property of their parents. They were a tangible example of a meek member of society, and clearly the disciples needed a healthy dose of meekness that day.

Now let's turn our attention to the word *welcome.*

In your own words, what does it mean to really welcome someone or something into your heart?

_____

_____

_____

_____

_____

Welcoming something means you need to *make room for it.* Often we welcome people in by opening a door or pulling up a chair, but how can someone be welcomed if the door is blocked or the table is full? This is the gist of what Jesus said here—you cannot properly welcome the ways of the Lord into your heart if it is crowded with all the wrong things!

Pride, bitterness, and fear keep us from welcoming people and ideas into our hearts and lives. Jesus challenges us to surrender, reminding us that He is guiding us as we welcome new and better things into our lives. It's obvious to us that the disciples' pride led to bitterness and arguing as they each attempted to elevate themselves. We probably can easily agree with Jesus that they needed to chill out.

But what about the bitterness in your own heart?

Imagine that you're sitting in your room, scrolling through your Instagram, and your eyes focus on an image of a pretty girl. She's got *the* body, *the* face, and *the* style. The comparison and jealousy quickly consume you. Right as you're about to insult her in your mind, Jesus reminds you to keep your eyes focused on Him, not others.

Imagine you feel a nudge to stop and talk to someone on the street and tell them about your faith. You decide to push that feeling away, because this person is dirty, smelly, and definitely not someone you would usually associate with. Jesus is next to you, reminding you of that little child.

Do you need a heart check just as badly as the disciples did that day?

Later on in this chapter, Jesus says to "be at peace with each other" (v. 50). That person you're jealous of, the new girl your ex is dating, the classmate or colleague you constantly compete with and compare yourself to—are you at peace with them? Is it really about them or is it about the fears, insecurities, and bitterness they trigger within you?

Have you really made room in your crowded heart to love them?

What stops us from living out our faith like children, full of awe and wonder? This week we get to engage in a serious heart check. Let's root out our bitterness and replace it with love, just like Jesus asked His disciples to do all those years ago.

Nelleke's Story

NELLEKE MEERMAN GRADUATED FROM CALIFORNIA LUTHERAN UNIVERSITY AND SERVED AS THE WEST COAST REGIONAL DIRECTOR FOR DELIGHT WHILE RUNNING HER OWN PHOTOGRAPHY BUSINESS (CAN YOU SAY BOSS LADY?!). SHE IS TRULY A BEACH GIRL AT HEART, SPENDING HER FREE TIME SWIMMING IN THE OCEAN AND TAKING LONG NAPS IN THE SAND. NEL IS YOUR GO-TO THERAPIST FRIEND, ALWAYS DOWN FOR A DEEP CONVO ABOUT FEELINGS, DOGS, OR BOTH.

As a ten-year-old, I loved my Saturday routine with my dad—hanging out in his little apartment, eating turkey sandwiches by the pool, and listening to him read *Harry Potter* out loud. I loved watching a movie every Saturday night and then waking up to hurry across town for church, with toast in hand (punctuality has never been my father's strong suit). Church was always followed by time at the beach. It was a simple routine, but one that brought much needed predictability in my life.

When I was eleven, my dad introduced me to a woman he was dating and her five-year-old son. Quickly our routine shifted to accommodate these two newcomers. Then when I was thirteen, one Saturday morning in December, my dad sat me down and told me that he was moving to Colorado, and that he was going to ask his girlfriend to marry him.

Wait...what?

What about me? I stay in California? And see you a few times a year?

So many questions flew through my mind, but I didn't know what to say or how to feel. Like many people, I cherished predictability and control, and in that moment I knew everything was going to change. We couldn't have our routine if he lived states away from me! For a while I felt completely numb. People we knew shared their opinions and congratulations, and I nodded and smiled—feeling defeated but unsure of how to process everything.

Eventually, the wedding rolled around. They got married in the church my dad and I went to every Sunday. I burst into tears as the ceremony came to an end and hid in the bathroom. People came up to me and said it was so sweet how emotional I got, but they didn't understand that it wasn't for a sweet reason at all. I felt abandoned, unwanted, and unworthy. In my thirteen-year-old mind, my dad's career and new family were important to him, and I didn't matter at all.

As months passed, my anger grew. I was so hurt by my dad, and it felt like he had deserted me. Eventually my resentment was replaced by jealousy and anger toward my stepbrother. I had to *lose* my dad, but my stepbrother got to *live* with him! They weren't even really father and son! He was *my* dad and mine only! Visiting them in their new home was painful for me. It was hard to see my dad's new life and feel like I had no place in it. I felt worthless.

Feelings of worthlessness are often accompanied by feelings of disappointment, anger, bitterness, and envy. This is a rough combination, a mixture that so many of us have felt in our lives. Even though we heal and grow, that pain is still a part of our story. This means that we're vulnerable to things that trigger the part of us that was deeply hurt.

1. Bitterness gets in the way of the freedom God has for you.

It took me a long time to realize how unfair it was to put all of this bitterness and resentment on my stepbrother, on people who had happily married parents, on friends who had great relationships with their fathers, and on my dad. My bitterness wasn't about them, it was about what I believed their actions said about *me*. It was about my lack of self-worth.

I didn't learn this lesson until this past year, but I hope you'll remember this: **it is not about them.**

I didn't have room in my heart to love them the way God was calling me to, because it was too full of my own hurt. Ask God to show you what your bitterness is really about. Could you be getting in your own way of healing? He wants to give you those answers and lead you to deeper understanding and compassion—toward yourself and others.

My bitterness toward my dad was about my feelings of abandonment, and my fears of being forgotten and seen as unimportant.

My bitterness toward my stepbrother was rooted in jealousy. He wasn't any greater or better than me—we are all created equally. But I wanted something that he had. That feeling was rooted in insecurity and not feeling worthy of the thing I so desperately wanted: for my dad to be close by and to feel like *my* dad.

My bitterness toward people who had happily married parents (and in my mind, had never gone through something hard) was rooted in feeling invalidated, like no one honored my pain and no one understood me.

Can you see the trend here? All of these feelings that I focused on, though rooted in things that really hurt me and desperately needed healing, stood in the way of my freedom. Just like the disciples who couldn't understand Jesus's point because they were too distracted by their toxic comparisons, I too was caught in an emotional storm that clouded my vision of reality.

2. God can use bitterness to reveal our crowded hearts.

I don't think for one second that Jesus was surprised to hear that the disciples had been arguing about who was the greatest. God *always* knows what's going on. So why did He let it happen? Why didn't He cut the argument off the second it started? Maybe at that moment, when He stopped His disciples and sat them down for a teaching moment, He had us on His mind. Maybe He could picture your struggle, your own crowded heart, and He wanted to give you the way out. Our God will never waste an opportunity to bring His children back to His feet. Sometimes, He uses trials to bring good.

If I'm being honest, on top of the feelings I harbored toward my family, I also experienced bitterness toward God. I was angry at Him for not giving me the life I wanted, the life I thought I needed to be happy and content. As time went on, there were many moments when I thought I knew better than God. I tried to take control out of His hands, not trusting Him to do it right. At the root of that lack of surrender is fear; sometimes it's scary to admit how much we need God and His love.

I kept trying to figure out what was most important to my dad. *Was it his career? Money? His new family? Or was it me?* The truth is, my dad did what he thought was best. As an adult, I can see why he made that choice and I also can see how it has shaped our family. We are all broken people, and our decisions affect the people around us for better or for worse.

"For all have sinned and fall short of the glory of God."
Romans 3:23

The disciples were not always welcoming. They didn't always make room for love. Even after this pep talk from Jesus, we see them continue to mess up time and time again. But the beautiful thing is that God still used them. That's the wonder of the gospel. You are never too far gone and never out of God's reach.

My dad's actions hurt me. As I've gone through life, others have hurt me too. I have experienced pain, heartbreak, and trauma. But I can tell you with 100% certainty that God never abandoned me or left me to deal with my pain alone. He provided me with a shoulder to cry on *and* the tools I needed to clear out the bitterness from my heart.

3. Servant-hearted posture clears out a crowded heart.

Remember what Jesus said after catching His disciples in their bitter, distracted moment?

"Anyone who wants to be first must be the very last, and the servant of all."
Mark 9:35

Truly welcoming someone into your heart means serving them and checking your pride at the door. Humility is so powerful and so freeing!

Loving others is not always easy. It is a choice. A choice to lay down your pride and allow others to break down your walls. A choice to accept a person for all that they are, not only the parts that we like or benefit from. Loving my family even though their decisions have hurt me is something that I have to choose sometimes. There are days when loving them is effortless, and days when I have to lay things down to love them—a part of being imperfect and human.

Loving others leads to freedom. Freedom from bitterness, from pride, from insecurity. Accepting others just as they are also allows freedom to accept yourself in your imperfection.

Bitterness gets in the way of forgiveness, and takes away your peace—which is too valuable to give up! The good news is that God transcends the hurt and bitterness, and guides us as we heal and grow.

It's okay that we relate to these disciples, too caught up in our own drama to see the hand of the Lord in our lives. God can offer us a way out. Recenter with Him today. Clear out your crowded heart and make some room. He *will* fill you up in the way that you have been craving.

He's just that good.

Conversation Starters

+ How did this week help you know yourself in a new way?

_____

_____

_____

_____

_____

_____

+ Fill in the space below with what is currently crowding your heart. Is it bitterness, comparison, pride? Be honest with yourself.

+ After taking inventory of what is really going on in your heart, what do you need to get rid of to make room for Jesus?

_____

_____

_____

_____

_____

_____

+ Nel talks about the power of a servant-hearted posture. What would it look like to take that on in your daily life and relationships?

_____

_____

_____

_____

_____

_____

"Loving others leads to freedom."

03

Notes

Notes

PART THREE

Make Jesus Known

Okay, now we're getting emotional. This has been an incredible journey so far and the end is in sight. Welcome to section three of KNOWN: Make Jesus Known.

"Therefore go and make disciples of all nations, baptizing them in the name of the Father and of the Son and of the Holy Spirit, and teaching them to obey everything I have commanded you. And surely I am with you always, to the very end of the age."
Matthew 28:19-20

When we know Jesus, everything changes. There is not a corner of our hearts and lives that His power doesn't reach. But those changes are not just for us—they are also for the people that don't know Him yet. In the Great Commission, Jesus gave us all a job: Go and make disciples. We are not called to be complacent, letting life pass us by. We are called to be in it, winning hearts for the Lord and telling everyone the Good News of the gospel.

Does that sound like a big task? Don't worry! God gives us all the tools we need.

Be an Influencer

THIS WEEK WE WILL LEARN HOW TO MAKE JESUS KNOWN BY USING OUR INFLUENCE FOR HIS GOOD PURPOSE! WE ARE THE SALT AND THE LIGHT FOR THIS WORLD!

Okay. It's Week 8 of Known, and it's time to ask the real questions.

Would Jesus have an Instagram?

Would He have more followers than Kim Kardashian?

Would Jesus follow *your* Instagram?

Furious scramble to delete thirst traps and Drake lyrics.

You know we're just messing around! But seriously, there is so much freedom and excitement in knowing that our worth and identity is not found in our follower count, the school we go to, our relationships, friendships, church attendance, political affiliations, mistakes, and more. We get our worth from Christ alone—and knowing and believing that truth changes everything! When we really know ourselves, we can go make Jesus known.

This week, we are going to read one of Jesus's most powerful and influential teachings—the sermon that would have gotten more views on YouTube than Justin Bieber's "Baby" music video. Any guesses on what this message is called? Hint: Jesus taught it from the top of a mountain...

Ding, ding, ding! The Sermon on the Mount. This is the longest recorded sermon by Jesus, a total of three chapters which are found in Matthew. We won't be breaking down every verse of this sermon (sigh of relief) but we are going to focus our attention on what Jesus said God's plan is for believers.

Go ahead and take a quick glance through Matthew 5.

Before we jump right in, it's important to fully understand what happened leading up to this moment. Jesus had just been baptized by John the Baptist, fasted in the wilderness for forty days while being tempted by Satan (look back at Week 5 to refresh your memory), and began His mission in Galilee. Matthew 4 shows us how Jesus healed every kind of sickness and preached the Good News of God's kingdom. This good news spread rapidly, which is why large crowds from Galilee, the Decapolis, Jerusalem, Judea, and the region across the Jordan gathered to seek Him and listen to Him speak. Keep in mind that this massive crowd consisted of His disciples, common folk, and Pharisees. There was not a single person outside of Jesus's invitation to receive God's grace and follow Him.

Picture being a part of this crowd of people who gathered with Jesus on that hillside. Imagine Him looking you in the eyes and saying, "You are My plan."

What thoughts immediately come to mind? Are you tempted to feel unqualified to be a part of His work?

_____

_____

Jesus was trying to reach the *hearts* of the people. There were many people in the crowd who put their faith in the law in order to get to heaven, but what Jesus was trying to explain here challenged the beliefs they had upheld for most of their lives. Imagine what went through their minds as Jesus explained that He was the fulfillment of the Law—that no amount of sacrifices or rituals would get them to Heaven. This was heavy stuff for the people who were there. Let's see what happened next!

Stop and read Matthew 5:13.

"You are the salt of the earth. But if the salt loses its saltiness, how can it be made salty again? It is no longer good for anything, except to be thrown out and trampled underfoot."

We are...the salt of the earth? Is Jesus *seriously* comparing us with the thing we put on our eggs in the morning? At first glance it may seem so, but it's actually a lot deeper than that. (Most of the things Jesus says have a deeper, hidden meaning that we need to pay close attention to!) He is actually giving us a mission. In this biblical context, salt would have been used as a *preserving agent,* used to preserve meat so it wouldn't rot. For us, this means we get to preserve and persevere in the faith, making sure that the kingdom of God will last throughout the ages. We are

His ambassadors, reminding the world of God's undying and unspoiling promise of salvation. What an honor!

So why else does Jesus want us to be like salt? Well, we know that salt adds flavor, so we should too! Our lives should not be bland, boring, tasteless or, well—saltless. They should be the very opposite, because Jesus says that without our flavor, we are good for nothing! We get to show the world what life looks like with Jesus! We are the salty influencers to a world that has gotten used to rotten meat.

Have you ever thought that being a Christian meant that you would have a boring life? Why do you think people hold on to that assumption?

_____

_____

_____

_____

_____

_____

Now, go ahead and drink some water if you're feeling a little parched from this talk about salt, and let's take a look at Matthew 5:14-16.

Fill in the blanks on the following page.

"You are the _____ ____ _____ _____ *. A*
town built on a hill _____ ____ _____ *.*
Neither do people light a lamp and put it under
a bowl. Instead they put it on its stand, and it
gives light to everyone in the house. In the same
way, _____ _____ _____ _____ _____
_____ *, that they may see your good deeds and*
glorify your Father in heaven."

What stands out to you in this passage of
Scripture?

In other words, Jesus calling us salt and light is essentially saying
that we are the plan for bringing about transformation in this
place!

Are we tracking here? YOU. ME. WE...are the light of this
world. So many people question the Lord's goodness and His
existence wondering why there is so much evil and darkness in
this world. Instead of directing this question toward God, we
should be asking ourselves, what are WE doing about all of the
darkness and evil in this world? Because God has already chosen
us, therefore we are called to go and shine the light. There are
no more excuses for people questioning the goodness of God
when He has already sent US. We are the walking, living, and

breathing image of God. We are the reflection of our creator. When people meet us, they should meet Jesus.

We pray these words are stirring in your heart right now. Sit for a second and recap these two very important things that God is calling us to be. Write them down here and reflect on the significance of our calling to be salt and bring light to those in darkness.

_____

_____

_____

_____

_____

_____

_____

_____

_____

_____

Brittney's Story

BRITTNEY STOBBIE KILLED IT AS DELIGHT'S SOUTHEAST REGIONAL DIRECTOR AFTER GRADUATING WITH A DEGREE IN EVENTS MANAGEMENT FROM THE UNIVERSITY OF FLORIDA. BRITT IS ONE OF A KIND! SHE'S SO FULL OF JOY AND HAS THE ABILITY TO MAKE ANY CONVERSATION HILARIOUS. SHE CAN FREESTYLE RAP LIKE NOBODY'S BUSINESS AND WILL NEVER TURN DOWN A CUTE PHOTO OPPORTUNITY.

Hey y'all! My name is Britt. I'm so excited to share a little bit of my "influence" story!

I want to set the scene for us here. The year is 2012. Many people believed the world was going to end, so this adds some spice. But rather than the world ending, something really huge was just beginning, and I was in middle school when I began to play a part in it. Any ideas what I'm talking about? Ah, yes, the rise of social media. I'm excited to give you a little glimpse of my story and show you how God has been working in my heart and in my life, and the things He has been revealing to me not only about Himself, but myself too—because the more that we know God, the more we know ourselves.

I cannot think of a better time to chat about influence, because it seems as if everyone is influenced by something, whether we acknowledge that we are or not. First, let's take a look at the definition of influence: as a verb, influence typically means to affect or alter by indirect or intangible means. Something or someone that influences a person or thing, then, has an influence on that person or thing.

Before we go any further, write down 3 major influences in your life.

1. _____

2. _____

3. _____

I vividly remember posting pictures on Instagram with Shawn Mendes and Cameron Dallas (throwback to the MAGCON days—if you know what I'm talking about, you're an OG) and getting a lot of likes on a few pictures and even being noticed by Cam himself. Oh, to be seen, known, and recognized by a celebrity when you're 14...it's hard not to get all giddy and excited.

It was in one of these moments when I realized that my sense of identity and validation was not coming from the Lord, but instead, from people using an app which had begun to feed my self-worth. If you don't know already, compliments and likes (from friends or strangers) are a poor diet to live on.

Shoutout to Jesus for helping a freshman in high school realize that and take it upon herself to get rid of all her social media. I deleted it all: Instagram, Snapchat, Twitter, and Facebook, and I never looked back. Every time someone would ask for my username, I'd have to explain that I didn't have an account. The reaction was the same, time and time again—they'd gasp in disbelief, say something along the lines of, "Wow, I could never do that. Good for you!" Some people actually thought I was lying. That is how strong of an influence social media has on people—it is literally unbelievable for someone our age to not take part in it.

Looking back, I truly feel confident in saying that I never battled any major feelings of insecurity or questioned my self-worth. This is because I had a firm foundation built on the Word of God and this ingrained truth of my identity being in Christ alone. I am who *He* says I am, not what an app thinks of me or what culture says I should be. All throughout high school and college I loved being the girl that wasn't on Instagram. I really do believe my relationship with Jesus grew stronger because I was filling my time seeking Him and began to put my full identity in Him; however, looking back, I can see how bitterness started to take root and my heart became prideful (which is pretty ironic since I prided myself in not being prideful). *Yikes.* I can't help but think of missed opportunities to love the people that God placed in my life in that season because I was too focused on myself, and too occupied with being "set apart" and different, that I almost missed the point entirely: to go and love the people around me.

I'll just get straight to the point: by choosing not to take part in what I called "the devil's playground" a.k.a. social media (I know how harsh that sounds, but that was truly my judgement), I ended up putting myself on a pedestal. I was no different than a Pharisee, looking down on others and making myself feel righteous, when really I should have been considering others above myself (Philippians 2:3).

I made a promise with the Lord and told Him that I would never get an Instagram unless He told me to, specifically, for work purposes. Fast forward to August 2020 when I became a Regional Director for Delight—my boss broke the news that I would have to get an account again. I still felt super cautious about it but asked God to make it extra clear if this was okay with Him. That's when He spoke Matthew 5:14 to me. He made it so clear that I was not to dim my light, that I was to go and be a light to this world, in this way, during this time.

Although this is my personal story, I want to encourage you to ask the Lord what He may be leading you to do with your use of social media. Maybe you need to set a time limit when you're on your phone, unfollow some accounts for your own well-being, or maybe you need to quit cold turkey because it's not doing your relationship with the Lord and others any good. Or, maybe you're like me, and you have been off the grid for a while. If so, ask God to give you wisdom in this area and direct your steps.

1. There is always something we can't see influencing something we can.

In other words, Scripture puts it like this:

"For our struggle is not against flesh and blood, but against the rulers, against the authorities, against the powers of this dark world and against the spiritual forces of evil in the heavenly realms."
Ephesians 6:12

This is one of my favorite verses in the Bible because I believe it holds so much power to transform our thoughts, actions, and lives.

We can either let social media (or insert what you wrote for whatever has influence over your life) consume and control us, or we can use it as a God-given platform to shine and be a light in an atmosphere that can sometimes be so very dark and toxic. We can use it to honor our bodies, other people, and God. Instead of viewing it through a negative lens, I started to see it as a gift and opportunity to live out this verse in Matthew.

"Let your light shine before others, that they may

see your good deeds and glorify your Father in heaven."
Matthew 5:16

Delight has a sister ministry called For the Girl. One of my favorite things that this ministry does is a podcast where the founders, Mac and Kenz, teach on hot topics for Christian women. In one podcast episode, Mac said, "The places we don't occupy, the enemy will." This has really stuck with me, as this doesn't just relate to social media but to everything in life.

2. You are only as loving as you are toward the person you love least.

This passage challenges me to recognize I am only as loving as I am toward the person I love least. I remember sitting in my seat at church when my pastor said that, and my jaw dropped to the floor. How have I never heard that before? I immediately felt so much conviction as I began to list people in my head to whom I knew I wasn't showing Christ's unconditional love.

Think about that person in your life. Maybe it's your roommate, a coworker, or a family member that you have a hard time liking, let alone *loving*. If only we could see what God sees! If we only knew all the behind-the-scenes footage, I think we all would have a lot more compassion for one another. This is why it's so important to pray to have God's eyes and an eternal perspective. This is also why I believe one of the most powerful things we could pray is this: *God, give me a deeper love for them.* This prayer actually holds power to transform our hearts, thoughts, and attitudes toward people.

Let's not just keep this in our heads.

Write down the names of people that come to mind. Pray over them and let's begin to see the Lord completely give you a new heart and sense of love for them.

_____

_____

_____

_____

_____

This is certainly something that Satan does not want us to pray for. Why? Because the truth will be revealed to us. Because when we earnestly pray for the Spirit to help us love someone, the Spirit actually transforms our heart, and we forget about the record of wrongs. Instead, we realize the real enemy was never other people, but Satan himself.

I want to be very clear that the negative influence that social media can have is not just due to our nature as sinful human beings—although that does play a role in it—but as children of God, we have a very real enemy who comes to kill, steal, and destroy. This is why it is important to realize the calling of being the salt of the earth.

"But if the salt loses its saltiness, how can it be made salty again? It is no longer good for anything, except to be thrown out and trampled underfoot."
Matthew 5:13

As believers, if we lose our salt, our preserving agent, we could also lose our sense of identity in Christ.

3. The biggest indicator of how much influence Jesus has in your life is how well you love other people.

Jesus said:

"By this everyone will know that you are my disciples, if you love one another."
John 13:35

Sounds easy, right? If so, why is it so hard for Christians to love the people that need this love the most? The way we love others shows the world who we are, and that, ultimately, will reflect the love of God.

Many people claim to follow Jesus, but their speech, deeds, and actions may show otherwise. I don't want this moment to pass without us doing a serious heart check and taking a look at our lives from the outside. Because having a Bible verse in our Instagram bio or posting a story of the devotional we're reading for the sole intention of getting praise or recognition is not what being a disciple of Jesus is. Our intentions behind these actions should be to bring life to our followers and do every single thing for His glory. Of course our deeds and our works are not what save us either; however, Matthew tells us that the way people know we belong to Jesus is by being the salt of the earth and the light of the world.

Salt and light are visible evidence that we have been transformed by our personal relationship with Jesus. If we call ourselves disciples of Jesus but people see us as negative, judgemental, angry, harsh, quick-to-speak, prideful, finger-pointing, stone-casting people, then why on earth would they want to follow Jesus? If His followers, who claim to be the people that know and love Him most, don't truly reflect the heart of Christ, why would anyone be interested in knowing *Him*?

Relationships are the key to influence. We will only have influence on that which we love. If we can *love* them (the world, our neighbors, our enemies) then we can have *influence*. Our relationship with our Father in heaven is the key to our influence in this world. Remember Jesus tells us this when He says that we are the *light of the world* and a city built on a hill *cannot be hidden*. When we are full of God's love, committed to embodying the salt of the earth, the world will notice.

When we know who we are as children of God, we get to remind people who they are! This is the greatest joy and honor: getting to tell people that the creator of this universe loves us so much that He took our place on a cross to pay the ultimate penalty for our sins, all because of His all-consuming, everlasting, unconditional love for us. So, let's not miss another opportunity to share this good news, and let's live out our identity that God has given us and go be the salt and light in this dark and hurting world!

Conversation Starters

+ How did this week equip you to go make Jesus known?

_____

_____

_____

_____

_____

_____

+ What is the biggest thing in your life that influences you
other than Jesus?

_____

_____

_____

_____

_____

_____

+ Be honest—how well are you representing Jesus to the people you meet? Who do you need to do a better job at loving?

|———————————|———————————|———————————|———————————|

TERRIBLE   BEEN   IT'S OFF AND   I TRY!   IT COMES
         BETTER...   ON!   NATURALLY

_____

_____

_____

_____

+ What do you tangibly need to do to allow Jesus to influence your life more so that you can be a brighter light to the world around you?

_____

_____

_____

_____

_____

_____

_____

"We will only have influence on that which we love."

Notes

Don't Miss Your Moment

WEEK NINE - MARK 14:32-42

THIS WEEK WE WILL LEARN HOW TO MAKE JESUS KNOWN BY STAYING VIGILANT AND READY TO RECEIVE HIS DIRECTION FOR OUR LIVES!

We have all been there—that feeling of scraping emptiness when you realize you missed it. Whether it's just one point away from an A, a second away from a PR, or a round away from that final interview.

You're holding your breath, only to let it out in slow disappointment.

When reading Scripture, it can be easy to dehumanize the people we hear about throughout the Bible. We think that they don't know what it feels like to lose. We read stories of seas parting and the sick being healed and it's easy to slip into the lie that the people in the Bible are different from us.

They don't struggle like I do.

They don't miss things like I do.

It's Week 9 of Known, and we are picking up this week with a story from Mark that puts these lies to death and reinforces the saving truth of the gospel: that Jesus came to save us all and that His Spirit continues to redeem us now.

Read Mark 14:32-42.

This passage is incredibly significant because of its nearness to the crucifixion. Here in this place called Gethsemane, we see the last moments of Jesus's freedom before He is arrested and taken away to the cross to die for the same people who hung Him there.

Gethsemane was a garden in Jerusalem located on the Mount of Olives. This place sat above sea level and had a beautiful view of the Holy City. The Mount of Olives is a significant place throughout Scripture—if you are a nerd for symbolism and love looking up the meanings of places, go look up this one!

In the beginning of this chapter, we see Jesus and the disciples walking into the garden. Disciples were the men Jesus chose to follow Him. (You can find their origin stories in the early chapters of Mark!) They were coming from what we know as the Last Supper and the weight of sorrow on Jesus was evident.

Fill in the blanks from Mark 14:34.

"My soul is overwhelmed with sorrow to the point of death," he said to them. "Stay here and _____ _____."

Jesus gave clear instructions to the disciples, and then He left to go be alone with God. He found a place away from them all and fell on the ground praying:

"Abba, Father..."
Mark 14:36a

Here we see the intimacy between Jesus and the Father. Abba is an Aramaic word for father and it was used by children, similar to "daddy" in English! Jesus was crying out for His dad to come to

Him. Picture Jesus in this moment sprawled on the ground, tears blurring His vision, barely sputtering out the words of His prayer. He knew what was to come, but despite His knowing, He still needed the comfort that only His heavenly Father could give. After this, He returned to the disciples and found them *asleep.*

There are moments in Scripture where we get a glimpse of the humanity of Jesus. His innate relational nature is on display here, and it seems He wanted to be comforted by His friends—to simply not be alone. Can we not relate to Jesus? We all can think back to a time when we were hurt, afraid, broken, and all we wanted was to be held, to be wrapped up in comforting arms and told that things were going to be okay. Clearly, the disciples missed the memo.

What did Jesus say to the disciples in verse 38?

Fill in the blanks below.

"Watch and pray so that you will not fall into _____. The spirit is willing, but the flesh is_____."

Jesus's character remained compassionate as He showed patience to His followers despite their disobedience. Jesus told them for the second time to keep watch, yet this time He added prayer to the mix. The disciples already had failed one attempt at keeping Jesus's command, but praise the Lord that we serve a patient, merciful God!

I love that Jesus always practiced what He preached. In this moment, Jesus had just come back from personal time with His Father in prayer, and He then told His disciples to do the same.

Pray.

We see here that prayer is not only the command by Jesus, but also the weapon. The key word in this first sentence of verse 38 is "so." Jesus told them to pray...*so* they would not fail again. Prayer is the weapon of choice for Jesus not only in His own struggle, but in the struggle of His people.

Right before going to the garden, at the Last Supper Jesus told the disciples how to pray. Part of that famous prayer holds these words in Matthew 6:13: "Lead us not into temptation, but deliver us from evil."

How often is prayer your first reaction to temptation or a struggle? Be honest!

_____

_____

_____

_____

This world offers us nothing but a beckoning into temptation and darkness. Part of the enemy's greatest schemes to take our eyes off Jesus is our own flesh. We see this play out in this story! Before the disciples and Jesus all entered the garden, the disciples were adamant that they would *never* abandon Jesus or deny Him! (Shoutout to my boy Peter!) Yet they all fell into their own fleshly desires not even hours later.

I believe most of us are like the disciples. We crave to be used by God in incredible ways—we sing worship songs with bold words full of surrender and lay down our own lives, yet we find ourselves asleep at the feet of Jesus. Where is the disconnect?

Verse 38 tells us.

"The spirit is willing, but the flesh is weak."

Write that again for yourself here.

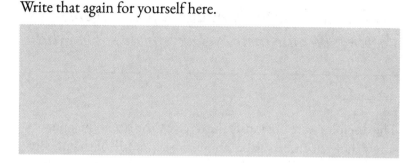

Until Jesus comes again, we will continue to be tempted by the world, the flesh, and the devil, and only through the power of the Holy Spirit can we fight this spiritual battle. As believers, we all have the Holy Spirit living inside of us, the same spirit that raised Jesus from the dead (Romans 8:11)!

However, the Spirit can only be activated by YOU. There's a famous preacher's line that says, "The Lord is a gentleman. He will not go anywhere He wasn't invited." What a way to think about our Lord! Imagine God just waiting, anticipating your invitation like a football team waiting for their moment to storm onto the field. This is a picture of the Holy Spirit in you!

The Spirit is simply God within us. The disciples had God with them in the form of the Son (Jesus) but not the Spirit. Let us not forget what a gift the Spirit is! It is ever present, a constant companion living inside of us.

The Lord is just waiting to reveal glimpses of His kingdom all around you, yet it takes us opening our eyes and staying awake, watching. From this story of the disciples, we know that in our own power we will fail, and we see the disciples fail for a second time.

Fill in the blanks from Mark 14:40.

"When he came back, he again found them sleeping, because their eyes were heavy. They did

_____ _____ _____ _____ _____ _____

_____ *."*

The disciples were obviously flustered by the situation, and surely they felt embarrassed, and maybe even full of shame. But now remember, the Holy Spirit was not on the scene yet. The Father sent the Spirit after the resurrection, so the disciples did not have the ability to call upon the Spirit for help!

But praise God, we do!

Let the disciples' failure be a call to action for us. They proved with all clarity that we can do *no* good thing apart from God—that we are desperate for His Spirit to help us. There are moments all throughout our lives that need a touch from the Father. Let us be the ones who invite Him to come and move!

We are all called to be a part of the Lord's mighty plan for redemption on this earth, which means staying alert and ready, always listening for His voice. When Jesus calls you into the unknown, will you be asleep on the ground or will you be firmly planted in His Word, attuned to His voice, and ready for action?

Don't miss your moment!

Carrie's Story

CARRIE BANTZ GRADUATED FROM MIAMI UNIVERSITY IN OHIO AND JUMPED INTO A REGIONAL DIRECTOR ROLE WITH DELIGHT WHERE SHE OVERSAW ALL OF THE DELIGHT CHAPTERS IN THE MIDEAST REGION. CARRIE IS ALWAYS DOWN FOR AN ADVENTURE AND LIKES TO START HER DAYS WITH LONG RUNS (WHILE LISTENING TO NPR). SHE IS AN AVID READER AND WRITER AND LOVES DEEP THEOLOGICAL DEBATES.

As humans I am convinced that we are all suckers for a good story, and a good story is made up of moments, the kind that prick your eyes with the threat of tears, or the ones that make the hair on your arms stand on end. I have always been one to become entranced by a story. I react the way the producers meant for their audience to react whether in the form of crying, gasping, or even yelling.

I am a self-acknowledged sucker.

This has played out in my life in the form of impulsion. I remember in my freshman year of college, I went to this campus ministry meeting where they showed a video of the place they were sending students on a summer mission for five weeks. I was *hooked*. I decided at that moment I was going to go to this foreign country I had never even heard of ten minutes before. I didn't know who else was going and I didn't know how I was going to raise the funds, but you better believe that I was *going*.

You probably read that and think I am a little insane, and I would agree with you. I tend to be one that *does* before she thinks. I am emotionally charged, hyped up, and totally on board with something, only to realize afterward that what I did was either 1) totally stupid; or 2) something I could not follow through on.

Does this sound familiar?

It's funny to think I am writing this story because I never realized (until now) how much I relate to the disciples in the garden. Remember how they were just coming from the last supper where they all said they would never abandon Jesus, yet in the garden they could not even stay awake for Him? The disciples had strong words, but weak actions.

Flashback to my junior year of college. I was on a spring break mission trip with that same organization I went with my freshman year. Our leader was giving a talk about ministry and how rewarding of a job it is to do after you graduate. Thinking back on this, there was a shift in me that I cannot explain except to say it was the Lord. My whole life I had been saying the *last* thing I wanted to do as a job was ministry (shoutout to all you pastor's kids who relate) and yet in that moment, I felt myself beginning to cry. I knew the Lord was changing me and calling me into something I would have never chosen by myself. I made a silent vow to the Lord that day, promising Him I would pursue ministry for at least a year post-grad.

1. The Lord will change your heart in order to prepare you for the ordained moments to come.

We serve a God whose purpose is to change us! We are daily being refined by the Holy Spirit in order to look more like Christ and less like our own flesh. What an equally exciting and terrifying thought!

What emotions come to mind when you think of being changed? Why do you think you feel that way?

My junior year came and went and before I knew it I was a senior at the career fair, mindlessly walking around clutching résumés and a whole lot of anxiety. The moment I had experienced months ago was tucked away in the depths of my memory, and I had fallen into my business school's mindset of success and security.

I sent in applications and attended first, second, and third round interviews, yet I found myself in January with nothing but rejection. I was defeated and directionless, spending a lot of time crying in my car. Part of me thought I had missed something and even if ministry was still on the table, I felt like I was too far on this path to turn back.

The enemy was building a prison of rejection around me, and I can't help but think the disciples must have felt similarly. When you feel like you fail God, there is not much that hurts more.

Both the disciples and I had clear paths set before us, yet we failed to follow through in our own power.

Around this time, the company I had been interviewing with the longest said no, and after three months of me putting all my eggs in that basket, I found myself thinking back to that moment on spring break. I remembered that Delight was hiring a team of Regional Directors to pour into Delight chapters. This was a full-time ministry position, a year straight of serving college women and raising the money to do so. Applications were out and I decided (as a *total* backup plan) to apply for Delight.

I could not have told you this before, but the rejection I was facing left and right was actually God *painfully* guiding me toward His will.

This is one of my favorite verses in the Bible because I believe it holds so much power to transform our thoughts, actions, and lives.

2. The Lord always provides a way because no one outruns His grace.

The Lord's saving grace ultimately results in us being united with Him for all eternity, so that grace in the *now* means He will continue to pursue us, no matter the conditions.

We see this in our story from Mark. After the disciples failed Jesus twice, He still went to the cross. The disciples' failure did not deter the Son of God's love and commitment to His people. Even throughout the Old Testament this remains true when God saves His people from starvation, slavery, and destruction.

His sovereignty has lasted through the ages and will continue through all eternity.

Human failure does not hold up.

I began interviewing for Delight and, to be honest with you, I was prepared to say no if they offered the position. I had convinced myself that this was not what the Lord had for me because it didn't *feel* right. I began praying that if Delight was my path, the Lord would have to break my heart for this ministry.

About a month later I got a call saying that the RD position was mine if I wanted it, and that I had a week to make my decision. Thus began my week of wrestling with the Lord, crying out to hear His voice and direction. Yet what I failed to realize was that He had already spoken direction over my life. I had just gotten caught up in the world around me.

Having the ability to look back on that time gives me the clarity to acknowledge that my lack of direction was not the Lord's fault, but the fault of my own stubborn heart. I was holding so tightly onto this idea of a corporate career that I was refusing the nudges of the Holy Spirit toward ministry. Sure, God calls so many people into so many different kinds of jobs, but He had called *me* to ministry, and I didn't want to listen. I knew the Lord had started a change in my heart, but I still had one foot in the world.

3. Having faith in both the world and the Lord leads to no faith at all.

I had faith that the world could give me something the Lord could not. Money, rest, comfort, and affirmation, to name a few. I had a divided faith, and it caused me to question whether the Lord could ever *really* fulfill my desires.

The direction of our faith drives how we react during the

significant moments throughout our lives, and a divided faith will lead us in the way of the world. Every single time.

Yet, in our struggle as old as Adam and Eve, the Holy Spirit still renews and the Lord still moves. My prayer continued to be for the Lord to break my heart for whatever He wanted me to do. On day four of my decision week I found myself in the psychology building on campus, crying for the women walking around my campus that were living in a constant state of emptiness.

The Holy Spirit had broken me.

Through the power of the Spirit, I was moved and burdened for these women. I found myself re-struck with the reality of not having Jesus: there are people walking around without hope, and that was their norm. Yet in that dark reality, the Lord was giving me a chance to get some skin in the game. He showed me that through Delight, I had the opportunity to help bring His daughters home.

The Lord had started a work in one little moment that had happened over a year before this and it was finally, fully coming to fruition through His spirit, despite my resistance.

This is only part of my story but one thing remains true: the Lord loves to plant me again and again on His path that leads to everlasting life. And no matter how many times the world pulls me from His path, He finds me.

Maybe unlike me, you're not trying to figure out whether to work in ministry or not. Maybe you're trying to decide what to do post-grad or maybe you're simply trying to figure out what clubs to get involved in or what internships to apply for. At every moment we have the choice to stay alert and ready to hear how God might be speaking—or we can easily fall asleep at the wheel and miss the Lord's direction and guidance for our lives. My guess is that God has something specific and purpose-filled for you in this season. He wants to use you, and I promise that His voice is calling out to you.

Will you listen?

Don't miss your moment! Stay alert for what the Lord is asking you to do next.

Conversation Starters

+ How did this week equip you to make Jesus known?

_____

_____

_____

_____

_____

_____

_____

+ Think back on a time when God had to change your heart. What did you learn?

_____

_____

_____

_____

_____

_____

+ What's the biggest thing you are trying to discern in your life right now? Be honest! How stubborn are you about getting your way in that area?

├──────────┼──────────┼──────────┼──────────┤

ROCK
SOLID

NOT LIKELY
TO CHANGE
MY MIND

MY MIND
COULD BE
CHANGED

I WANT TO
LISTEN TO HIS
VOICE

HIS WAY
OR THE
HIGHWAY

_____

_____

_____

_____

+ What is standing in your way from following God's calling on your life? How can you be ready when the moment comes?

_____

_____

_____

_____

_____

_____

_____

"Don't Miss Your Moment!"

Notes

Notes

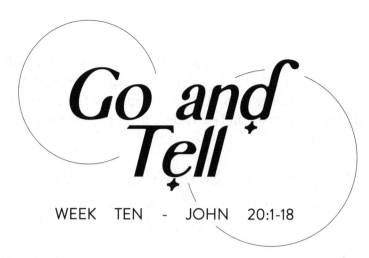

Go and Tell

WEEK TEN - JOHN 20:1-18

THIS WEEK WE WILL LEARN HOW TO PUSH PAST REJECTION AND STAY ON MISSION. WE ARE CALLED TO SHARE HIS GOSPEL WITH OTHERS, DESPITE ANY SETBACKS!

Welcome to Week 10, our last chapter in the Known book!
Over the last nine weeks we've spent time getting to know Jesus, learning how this allows us to truly know ourselves, and becoming equipped through the revelation of that knowledge to make the name of Jesus known to the ends of the earth. What a beautifully transformative journey it has been!

For our final week together, we want to look at the story of the resurrection. Let's see what happened in the aftermath of Jesus stepping out of the tomb and the specific commission He gave to one woman who walked closely with Him during His ministry.

Read John 20:1-10.

In John 20, we read that Mary Magdalene was up early before dawn en route to Jesus's tomb. Mary Magdalene is one of the most prominent women remembered from the life of Jesus. Be careful though, because she is not to be confused with Mary the mother of Jesus, or Mary the sister of Lazarus and Martha. Apparently Mary was a very popular girl name for the Jewish people—so it can all get a little confusing! Luke 8 tells us that Mary was a loyal follower of Jesus who traveled with Him proclaiming the Good News of the kingdom of God and even helped to support His ministry financially.

"Early on the first day of the week, while it was still dark, Mary Magdalene went to the tomb and saw that the stone had been removed from the entrance."
John 20:1

It's easy to brush past the first verse of John 20 and move on to the other more exciting parts of this story, but let's soak in the raw feelings of this moment. Mary was on her way to the burial place of Jesus. Can you imagine the weight of the emotions she must've been swimming in at that moment? Her beloved teacher had been crucified right in front of her (John 19:25). She could probably still picture the blood dripping down Jesus's side, the look on His face as He hung there in agony, the sound of His voice when He cried out His final words, "Tetelestai...It is finished" (John 19:30).

This was the man who saw value in her from the moment He laid eyes on her. This was the man who had understood her better than anyone ever had before. This was her Savior—the one who cast out the seven demons that had haunted and controlled her for so long (Luke 8:2).

Pause and think about who Jesus is to you. Write down 3-5 characteristics or ways that He has shown Himself faithful to you in the past.

_____

_____

_____

_____

_____

_____

This man who had utterly transformed Mary from *death to life* was suddenly gone. We can probably assume that every step she took that morning before getting to the empty tomb was full of deep sorrow and pain. Yet even in the midst of her mourning, don't you love that there was no place she would've rather been than at the resting place of her Lord? We know from the other Gospel retellings that Mary went to anoint Jesus's body with burial spices. She wanted to intimately worship and honor Him, even in His death.

When she arrived at the tomb, she saw that the stone sealing the entrance was not there. Immediately she turned to go and tell her friends that something was off. In verses 3-10 we see Peter and John (the author of this Gospel, the self-proclaimed "one whom Jesus loved") low-key competing to see who could get to the tomb first. When they arrived, they found the tomb empty just like Mary said it was. Peter and John decided to head back to their Airbnb in Jerusalem but our girl Mary stayed put at the tomb.

Read John 20:11-18.

We can't know for sure the thoughts that ran through Mary's mind in these moments. Maybe she thought that Jesus's body had been stolen, maybe she thought someone was playing a cruel joke on her, or maybe the weight of her emotions from the days before finally caught up with her in an instant. Mary sat there in the very raw feelings of her pain until something in her prompted her to look into the tomb once more. That's when she saw the angels!

Two angels dressed in white were sitting where Jesus's body had been. They addressed Mary and asked her why she was crying. It's not every day that angels appear out of nowhere. Like can you imagine?! What a roller coaster! She then spoke to the angels.

Fill in the blanks from John 20:13 below.

"They have taken _____ _____ away," she said, "and I don't know where they have put him."

Did you notice how Mary referred to Jesus as "my Lord?"

Not simply *the* Lord, or *the disciples'* Lord, or the Lord of Israel. Mary had such a deep kinship with Jesus that she felt comfortable referring to Jesus as *her very own*. This was a marker of an intimate and personal friendship. This wasn't religious, this was deeply relational.

At that moment another man appeared whom Mary mistook as the gardener. He asked her the same question and she begged him to help her find Jesus's body. That was until the man called her by name...

Jesus said to her, "Mary."

She turned toward him and cried out in Aramaic, "Rabboni!" (which means "Teacher"). John 20:16

One word changed *everything*. At the simple mention of her name, Mary knew that this was her Jesus. All of her sorrow, her confusion, and her pain were instantly redeemed. Isn't that just like Jesus to preach the *perfect* sermon in one word?

Although she had watched His very beaten, bruised, and bloody body be put in that tomb three days earlier (Matthew 27:61), here He was fully alive, standing in front of her. It didn't make sense, yet simultaneously it made perfect sense. Her Jesus was exactly who He said He was. He was the Messiah—the one they had all been waiting for. The one who had rescued her from darkness. The one who would keep His promises. The one whom even *death* could not defeat. This was the tangible power of resurrection!

What happened next is truly astonishing and beautiful, but it's easy to miss!

Fill the blanks from John 20:17.

Jesus said, "Do not hold on to me, for I have not yet ascended to the Father. _____ instead to my brothers and _____ them, 'I am ascending to my Father and your Father, to my God and your God.'"
John 20:17

Jesus told Mary not to cling to Him at this moment because she had other more important things to do. She was to "go and tell" about what she had witnessed outside of the tomb that day. Naturally, this might not seem like a big deal. But let's think about the magnitude of this moment: Jesus commissioned Mary Magdalene to be the inaugural carrier of the full gospel. She was the first person to witness the resurrected Jesus and the first one sent to "go and tell" others that Jesus was getting ready to ascend to be with His father in heaven!

This was unbelievably countercultural. Jesus chose to use a woman as the first eyewitness to His resurrection. But in that day and age, a woman's testimony was of no value. In the Jewish judicial system, a woman's word wouldn't even be accepted as concrete evidence!

It could've easily been Peter or John that Jesus chose to show Himself to first. It probably would've allowed more people to take it seriously from the jump! But Jesus chose a woman named Mary Magdalene with a spotted past and a less-than-perfect reputation to be the first carrier of His Good News into the world.

Don't you love Jesus and His upside-down kingdom? His ways don't always make sense to us but they are beautiful displays of His lavish love for us and His pursuit of *everyone's* heart.

What's an "upside-down" way that Jesus has shown Himself faithful in your own life or story?

_____

_____

_____

_____

_____

In verse 18 we see Mary respond in obedience to what Jesus had asked her to do. We're not sure how exactly she delivered the news but we can guess that it probably involved flailing arms, dancing feet, tear-soaked cheeks, and shouts of joy and praise. Her Savior was alive and nothing would stop her from telling everyone the Good News of Jesus. *He was alive!*

As we process what life looks like in light of the resurrection of Jesus, let's lean in this week to how Jesus might be calling each of us to "go and tell" the Good News of who He is and what He's done for us.

MacKenzie's Story

MACKENZIE WILSON IS ONE OF THE FOUNDERS OF DELIGHT MINISTRIES. SHE IS A PROUD ENNEAGRAM 8 AND LIVES IN CHARLOTTE, NORTH CAROLINA, WHERE SHE HELPS RUN DELIGHT AND FOR THE GIRL MINISTRIES. MAC IS A SELF-PROCLAIMED BIBLE NERD AND HAS A SECRET PAST AS A COUNTRY SINGER (CHECK HER OUT ON SPOTIFY)!

I'll never forget the moment. I was in the Delight office sitting in the big white chair with the tiny stain on the left armrest that we've never managed to get out. It took every ounce of strength in me to fight back the tears that were heavy on my eyelids—one blink and they would've all fallen in a dramatic instant.

The funny thing about rejection is that once you hear some sentiment of the words "you're not enough," everything else gets fuzzy from there.

I can't remember the exact details of what was said, the reasons why, or how I responded. All I remember was hearing two people I deeply respected and trusted tell me that I wasn't enough of a leader to continue running Delight at the level it had grown to. At this point in my life I hadn't experienced heartbreak like you see in the movies before, but I was pretty sure at that moment that this must've been it.

I could literally feel my heart drop. It ached.

Some guy wasn't breaking up with me. Someone wasn't saying they didn't love me back. I almost wish that would've been the case! Instead, the ministry that God led my best friend and me to start and to shepherd, the ministry that had personally changed my life, the ministry in which I had invested literal blood, sweat, and tears—felt like it was slipping through my fingertips.

Think back on your most recent memory of rejection. What did it feel like?

_____

_____

_____

_____

_____

_____

_____

All my friends know that I'm not much of a crier, and I'm typically far more led by logic than by my emotions. But for the next three months I couldn't stop crying. Every night I cried myself to sleep. Every time someone asked me how I was doing? I crumbled. Every day before work I would pause at the back door and wipe away a few stray tears before stepping foot back into the Delight office...the original scene of the heart-crushing crime.

One year after that initial comment, I was sitting backstage at the 2018 Delight Leadership Conference preparing to go out on stage and teach a message on the final night. It had been one year of living with the reverberating pain of a single moment of rejection. Tears, anger, confusion, frustration, doubt, pain, sorrow—you name it and I had felt it. But at the same time there had been sweet moments with Jesus, healing, joy, hope, confidence, powerful words spoken over me by people who believed in me, and a renewal of my identity as simply loved, seen, and chosen by my sweet Jesus.

But rejection has an uncanny power to perfectly interrupt every moment of security and contentment with echoes of past pain.

I so vividly remember pacing back and forth because it felt like the enemy was having a field day in my mind. The very two people who had spoken those words of rejection were going to be in the audience that night. I could feel their words haunting me as I tried to pray and prepare my heart to share what I felt God had put in me to impart to the women there that night.

1. Relationship breaks the sting of rejection.

I love that in our Scripture story from this week, we see Mary up early in the morning going to Jesus. She was facing unimaginable sorrow but even still, she went to find her Jesus. She didn't run from her pain or numb out with Netflix, oat milk lattes, online shopping, or some guy on Snapchat. Mary went to be with Jesus in the only way she could, even when the sorrows of the world were crushing her.

Now maybe she wasn't feeling the pain of someone telling her she wasn't enough, but Mary knew what it was like to be misunderstood, seen as an outcast, and tossed aside. That's why I think it's so powerful that she was the one still seeking out Jesus even after His death. Mary knew it was only her relationship with Jesus that had the power to redeem her pain.

When you're facing deep pain, what's the first thing you typically run to?

In that moment backstage I remember getting on my knees and pouring out my heart before Jesus, begging that He would give me the strength to make it through. To be totally honest? I wanted to get in my car, drive home, and leave my message for someone else to share.

But the beautiful thing about that moment is that despite the rejection, I was in relationship with Jesus—the only one who had and has the power to speak over and bring total healing to my deepest emotional, spiritual, and physical wounds.

You see, it's the power of relationship with Jesus that breaks the sting of rejection. It might not bring instantaneous relief, but it's the only thing that can truly treat and bring resolution to the sharpness of words and actions that cut the deepest parts of the soul.

At that moment, all I could do was 1) lean on my relationship with Jesus; and 2) remember His words.

2. Remember His words.

The Gospel writer Luke tells this resurrection story conversation from a slightly different angle that I want to look at together.

"In their fright the women bowed down with their faces to the ground, but the men said to them, 'Why do you look for the living among the dead?'"
Luke 24:5

In this retelling of the story, Mary was with a few other women at the tomb when the angels asked this simple yet profound question: "Why do you look for the living among the dead?"

Mary and her friends were looking for Jesus in the darkness of a graveyard, when He was already alive and walking in the light. So I want to ask you a similar question: *How many times have you looked for life in the tombs of dead men?*

In our culture today we're constantly looking for life and purpose in dead things. Fame, wealth, popularity, acceptance, sin, instant gratification, and relationships that don't spark life. So many of us wake up every morning, put on our Hokas, Nikes, or maybe Birks, and waltz right back to the graveyard of dead and decaying things looking for life yet again. We keep putting our faith in that relationship or friendship that will never fully satisfy. We continue chasing a dream, holding onto the idea that once we arrive we'll *finally* be happy. We sell our souls to the notion that "more" is the gateway to what we truly need.

In my own story, for a season I was romanced by the idea that maybe revenge or proving my haters wrong would bring the satisfaction that my heart needed. But I was so far from right! That was a dead end path that would only lead to more destruction and would never nourish my heart the way that Jesus could.

Name a "dead thing" that you've been looking to for life lately.

I pray that as women we stop looking for life among the dead, and instead find it in who Jesus is and what He has spoken over us. I love the second part of the angel's words for Mary and her friends:

"He is not here; he has risen! Remember how he told you, while he was still with you in Galilee: 'The Son of Man must be delivered over to the hands of sinners, be crucified and on the third day be raised again.'" Then they remembered his words.
Luke 24:6-8

The angels' second prompting to the women was to remember the things Jesus had already told them.

Okay, whoooaaaa. *That's powerful stuff right there!* Jesus told them that this would happen—He was to be crucified in Jerusalem but He would rise again.

Remembrance is so important in the face of rejection or deep pain. It's through holding onto the promises that Jesus has already spoken over us that we begin to find healing and peace. So I want to ask you:

What words of the Savior have you perhaps forgotten?
Which of His promises have you unknowingly stopped believing for yourself?
What truths have you relaxed for a more convenient alternative?
What commands are you deliberately choosing to not obey?

When Mary remembered what Jesus had already spoken, my guess is that it brought her a lot of peace and trust in that moment of deep pain and confusion. When we return to the Word and remember the promises of God, we leave space for Jesus to remind us of who we already are in Him.

As I cried out to Jesus that night backstage, I remember hearing a knock on the door. My friend Jana walked in and asked if she could pray for me. She laid hands on me and began to speak promise after promise over me about how my Father in heaven saw me—not because of my accomplishments, not because of my work ethic, not because of my personality, and not even because of my love for God, but simply because of my identity as His child.

3. Go and Tell!

Before Jana said "Amen" I knew that this was a direct answer to my prayers. Jesus was equipping me with His strength and Holy Spirit power to "go and tell" a room full of college women the same sweet message He had just whispered to me.

Like Mary that day outside of the tomb, I had important work to get to! I needed to "go and tell" people about the resurrection power of Jesus in my life and invite them into that same story.

I remember shedding a few tears that felt like the final tears of that long season, grabbing my Bible, and walking out commissioned, confident in who I was and what I was created to do.

Recently God has been breaking my heart in a new way for women of all ages. I see so many women deeply in love with Jesus but keeping the Good News of the gospel to themselves. They know Jesus and they know who they are in Jesus, but they aren't actively making Him known to others in their everyday lives.

I'm not sure what's holding them back. I'm not sure what might be holding you back.

Maybe it's a moment of rejection, maybe it's deep sorrow, maybe you don't feel like "enough," maybe you've never seen it modeled before, maybe you think that's reserved for pastors and leaders.

Name something that has been holding you back from sharing the Good News of Jesus with the world around you.

My prayer is that you would let Mary's post-resurrection conversation with Jesus be your commissioning. Mary and her friends were the first women to go and tell—even to those who didn't fully believe them at first and doubted their story. I don't know this for sure, but my guess would be that other people's reactions and rejections didn't stop them from telling people about their Savior, Teacher, and friend, because they were sent by Jesus Himself.

We see straight from Jesus that men and women alike have been charged with sharing the Gospel! Delight women, put your lamp on a stand, share about your Savior often, proclaim the Good News every chance that you get, and make Jesus known on every corner of your campus.

If you've never been told this before: You are a one-of-a-kind, divinely gifted disciple of Jesus. You have been commissioned and sent to "go and tell" others about not just a Savior, but *your* Savior. Remember who you are in Him, and make His name known to every single human being who will listen! Your story, your message, and your words are needed! ***Go and tell!***

Conversation Starters

+ How did this week equip you to go make Jesus known?

_____

_____

_____

_____

_____

_____

+ In her story, Mac was facing the sting of rejection. Is there anything in your life that you are currently mourning?

_____

_____

_____

_____

_____

+ Be honest, how often do you run to God's Word when you
are hurting? Why did you choose that answer?

|———————————+———————————+———————————+———————————|
I DON'T   IT HAS BEEN A   NOT MY FIRST   I USUALLY DO   ALWAYS IN
EVEN OWN A   WHILE   INSTINCT   THE WORD
BIBLE

_____

_____

_____

_____

+ How do you feel God specifically calling you to "go and tell"
about the Good News of Jesus?

_____

_____

_____

_____

_____

_____

_____

"Remember who you are in Him and make His name known."

Notes

Contributors:

Editing Team:
Content Edit by Maggie Sawler
Theological Edit by Aubrey Johnston
Editing by Represent & Co.

Story Writers:
Kaylie Peterson
Natalia Grace
Elysia Williams
Alex Meador
Maggie Sawler
Nelleke Meerman
Brittney Stobbie
Carrie Bantz
MacKenzie Wilson

Start a Delight

HELP US SPREAD THE WORD ABOUT DELIGHT!

There are thousands of college women all across the country that need Christ-centered community but have no idea Delight exists!!! We need women like you to help spread the word.

If this community has impacted your life in any way, don't you want to help other women experience it too?

If you know a friend who loves Jesus and who would make an amazing Delight leader–tell her about Delight! With just a few texts you could indirectly reach hundreds of college women on another campus!

How cool is that?!

www.delightministries.com

Point them to our website where they can sign up to bring Delight to their campus! Once they sign up, they will hear from us and will get everything they need to make this community happen at their university.

So... send a couple texts, call a couple friends, maybe post about it on your socials, and let's reach a million more college women together!

For more information, resources, or
encouragement head to...

WWW.DELIGHTMINISTRIES.COM